The Language of the Gods

by the same author
Hermes Unveiled

ROY NORVILL

The Language of the Gods

ASHGROVE PRESS, BATH

First published in Great Britain by
ASHGROVE PRESS LIMITED
19 Circus Place, Bath, Avon BA1 2PW

© Roy Norvill 1987

First published 1987

ISBN 0 906798 84 1

British Library Cataloguing in Publication Data
Norvill, Roy
    The language of the gods.
    1. Occult sciences   2. Initiations (in
    religion, folk-lore, etc.)
    I.   Title
    133   BF1442.I/

Photoset in 10½pt Bembo by
Ann Buchan (Typesetters), Middlesex
Printed and bound by Billings
Worcester

Contents

Preface

Those readers to whom the discovery and investigation of Hermetic allegory is a new experience will undoubtedly encounter in the following pages certain word and phrases, emphasised in an obviously meaningful manner, but which appear to lack sufficient explanation why. Indeed, some of them will *seem* to have been dealt with in a way that can only adequately be described as perfunctory.

To exempt myself from justifiable annoyance, I hasten to point out that, although this book has been designed to be comprehensible on its own, the real ground work by which the elusive segments may be more fully understood has already been extensively laid out in my book *Hermes Unveiled**.

Such is the all-encompassing scope of the expositions therein that total recapitulation here would have been counter-productive, annexing space now more advantageously utilised in the presentation of further revelatory research. I would respectfully suggest, therefore, that a browse through Hermes Unveiled would infinitely enhance appreciation of the present work.

---

* Ashgrove Press, Bath

Introduction

The mind of Man is capable of a certain, deliberate act of will, the successful application of which results in his being elevated to a higher state of consciousness, a realm of beneficence such as he has often dreamed of but never considered a reality.

Although every person possesses this hidden potential, none but a select number of each generation discover the means by which it may be activated. Even fewer, having made the discovery, actually accomplish the mental transformation to its highest degree.

As attainment of this much desired goal places at one's disposal powers that, if misapplied, can adversely affect the lives of others, Nature has imposed her own conditions upon the enrolling candidate. Thus, it can be confidently assumed that those who aspire to the transformation of consciousness are required, in the course of the process itself, to adopt higher principles of thought, incurring such a radical change in the normal psyche that the danger of misuse at the direction of the lower emotional self is eliminated.

Nevertheless, cognisant of the truth that, in Nature, everything is possible, the masters of the process were exceedingly careful in the way they dispensed knowledge of their experience to others. This powerful Science is not one that can be readily embraced by the unprepared mind unless a specific level of *understanding* has been reached; and history repeatedly attests to the grim fact that superstition, fear of the unknown, invariably leads to active persecution of the most violent nature.

Yet it was inconceivable that such a benefaction to mankind should remain unproclaimed.

Accordingly, with intellect sharpened by the very act of the process, the initiates devised a form of advertising which, while open to all eyes, would be understood completely only by those in whom the sense of intuition was greater than ordinary reason. This quality is admittedly rare, possessed by a lucky few, derided by the many. No wonder, then, that although the works of the initiates have consistently been thrust before their very eyes for generation after generation, century after century, the greater mass of the populace has remained blind to the real message so carefully contrived and directed at them.

Commonly, this method of encipherment is known by the term 'allegory', but in due deference to the wholly spiritual world to which it really refers, the initiates chose to call it the 'Language of the Gods'.

Chapter One

Allegorical works have this advantage; that a single word suffices to illumine connections which the multitude cannot grasp. Such works are available to everyone, but their significance addresses itself to an elite. Above and beyond the masses, sender and receiver understand each other. The inexplicable success of certain works derives from this quality of allegory, which constitutes not a mere fashion, but a form of esoteric communication.

(from the documents of the Priory of Sion – quoted in *The Holy Blood and the Holy Grail*, page 190)

To the thousaands who read the above quotation in the best-seller by Henry Lincoln and co-authors, the claim for existence of an allegorical code serving as an instrument of communication for a mysterious elite may have appeared wholly incredible, the more so in light of the statement that a 'single word' could evoke in the reader instant rapport with some scheme that lies beyond everyday comprehension. But such a code does exist, and has done since the time of the first written word. Before that it was to be found in the form of the hieroglyph, in symbols that carried in their fundamental, outward presentation, a second meaning to be interpreted only by those who possessed the mental key. And it is still true today that a 'single word' will do exactly what the allegorical writer expects of it, by unerringly diverting the attention of the knowledgeable from the literal sense of the text, directing it instead to an inner understanding, a great truth regarding human nature which may quite confidently be described as the Ultimate Science.

This Science, which employs neither mathematics nor machinery, demands no costly outlay from those desiring apprenticeship, for everyone already possesses the necessary qualification.

As to what this qualification is, the alchemists of the Middle

Ages, masters of the allegorical text, did not hesitate to describe in full:

> It is familiar to all men, both young and old, is found in the country, in the village, in the town, in all things created by God. Yet it is despised by all. Rich and poor handle it every day; it is cast into the street by serving maids; children play with it; no one prizes it; it is far, but also near at hand; it is the last, greatest and highest secret in Nature. . . .

Even a casual student of mediaeval Alchemy – from which collective sources these descriptions originate – will instantly recognise this sweeping but deliberately vague catalogue as having reference solely to that mysterious and much sought-after panacea, the Philosophers' Stone.

This 'stone' was, it is plain, not a stone at all. It was alternatively dubbed the Subject of the Wise, the First Matter and a thousand other titles, each one more misleading than its predecessor; accurate identification by those outside the knowledge was thus rendered well nigh impossible. But we give grateful thanks to certain writers, a compassionate few who at different periods of time saw fit to draw aside the veil gradually, allowing the discerning seeker an inlet to the truth. From them we can be assured that the object is correctly named.

It is that quality of mind known to us all as the *pure consciousness*.

The Dual Self

Any hope of understanding the allegorical language, not to mention the reason for its invention, rests upon adequate comprehension of the process by which the human mind functions, together with a subsequent realisation of the possibilities such knowledge unfolds. The term 'pure consciousness' employed above to describe the Philosophers' Stone is deliberately chosen and is intended to convey the idea of a simple state of self-awareness, totally unmarred by thought, imagination or emotion. It is, to portray it in even more plain words, the fundamental 'I' feeling within each mind, a recognition of Self before such time as any thought has intervened to identify it with an external situation. And this is a point which calls for further, very careful clarification, for the sensation of 'I' within is present in a dual role. One is well known to us, the other is concealed.

When we normally think of 'self', we do so in conjunction with our outward character, the personality evolved by habits and emotions practised and acquired during a lifetime. We tend to say 'I don't like this . . .', or 'I was annoyed because . . .', inferring the use of thought and emotion in the projection of our outward character – and indeed, our personalities could not exist without such mental accoutrements. But the concealed 'I' is totally impersonal, devoid of any acquired emotional characterisation, and can only be discovered either accidentally or by an act of will continually applied over a lengthy period of time. It is the *real* 'I', and as the allegorical writers went to such extreme lengths to conceal it, perhaps it would be wise to assume that its discovery would be a most desirable thing. As Madame Blavatsky remarked:

> There is much more contained in this language than we are willing to explain, but we will say that the secret is worth the seeking.
>
> (*Isis Unveiled*, Vol I, page 256)

This *formless matter*, however, the real 'I' to which Madame Blavatsky was referring, lies just beyond our normal senses of perception, or to be more accurate, heavily concealed by the same. Accidental revelation of this impersonal Self may occur at moments of great stress or shock, when all thoughts are momentarily frozen. Afterwards, this phenomenon is usually described in the common phrase; 'my heart stood still'. In truth, it is the act of thought which is entirely suppressed for a few seconds of time, not the physical heart-beat. An event of this nature makes a deep impression on the mind of the recipient, not solely in response to the external cause, but because the usually unbroken activity of the thought-stream is suddenly and rudely stopped in its tracks. This unprecedented mental standstill, with its few seconds of utter *silence* in the mind, effectively reveals that *consciousness can exist without thought*.

Normally, such a concept is not likely to occur to the rational, outward thinking mind, for knowing that thought is necessary as an energy behind every motor activity, it is assumed that the process of thinking must have continuity if the human machine is to remain functional. Thus we are habitually tolerant of the 'internal dialogue', the incessant parade of ideas, decisions, opinions, sensations and imaginings that flit across the mental sphere, even whilst the physical body is at rest, and we are deluded into believing that we have them under perfect control. To demonstrate the error of this assumption all that is required is the memory of an experience familiar to all at one time or another – those nights in bed when one lies twisting and turning in exasperation, while an over-active and totally uncontrollable mind effectively prevents the onset of sleep.

And somewhere behind the 'clamour' of the thought-stream lies the source of its power, the pure consciousness, an energy which cannot be reached by the outward mind until the itinerant thought activity has been subjugated by the will.

In order that the differing functions of thought and consciousness may be more fully appreciated, it may be helpful to present the analogy of an electric motor which powers a machine shop lathe. To operate the lathe, we switch on the mains supply which, by its passage through the coils of the motor windings, produces a second energy in the form of a magnetic flux. It is this new force that turns the motor armature, not the mains current on its own, thus producing a physical motion transmitted in turn to the chuck of the lathe. Note, then, that there are two similar but entirely separate forms of energy involved – the mains current itself, and the magnetic flux created by the coil windings in the motor. When we switch off the motor, the magnetic flux ceases to exist, but the mains current is still present at the other side of the switch, waiting to be drawn upon.

In the case of the human mind, the the mains supply is the pure consciousness, the magnetic flux the process of thought, and the lathe representative of the physical body. When we wake up in the morning, 'current' is immediately drawn and the thought process begins. In turn, this sets the physical body in motion. The reason for presenting this analogy is to make the point that, when operating a lathe, we switch off the motor whilst the machine is being set up for work, thus allowing the mains current to be used elsewhere if necessary. And we do not walk away leaving the lathe motor turning idly. In the human mind, however, consciousness is being continually drawn upon, even at times when the physical body is at rest and no immediate project is engaging our attention. So habitual is the incessant continuity of the thought-flow that, even before we reach adulthood, we have lost the power of resting in self-awareness alone until thought activity is required. Thus the mind is never quiet. We can no longer switch off the 'magnetic flux'.

The result of this perpetual wastage is that we are prevented from discovering the other powers of the pure consciousness.

The Dual Consciousness

For the lay person, material knowledge and experience of the mind powers has led to its common division into two separate aspects. The first and the most obvious is the ordinary, everyday function of the mind in the material world. We call this the *conscious mind*, and it consists of those qualities familiar to our lives: thought, emotion, memory, imagination, and the rest. The second is much more of an enigma and appears to be a doorway to that region of the unknown, the Paranormal, for research has repeatedly shown its limits to be far in excess of those within which the conscious mind operates. This second aspect has become loosely known as the *subconscious mind*, an unfortunate error of nomenclature, for it is a higher intelligence than the conscious mind, rather than a lower. To avoid confusion, however, I will retain the term, using it at times in place of the original 'pure consciousness'.

The reason why the Philosophic Stone of the subconscious was so carefully concealed in allegory is because it is the seat of creative power. In the material world, we are from time to time given some tantalising glimpses of this supreme energy. In certain individuals under specific conditions, we have witnessed, recorded and filmed seemingly impossible phenomena – calculative abilities, total recall, instantaneous telepathic communication across vast distances, prevision, and even, in the case of poltergeist activity and stigmata, the subconscious manipulation of both inert and animate matter. Countless documentations attest to such events and I assume the reader to be well enough acquainted with them to make it unnecessary for me to catalogue them further.

More to the immediate point, I move on to emphasise that the two common factors described, the conscious and the subconscious, are not to be confused with the activity of the two lobes of the brain.

Long ago, medical science provided us with the information that the brain consists of two separate lobes, mounted under the left and right sides of the skull. More recent research has revealed that although each lobe has its specific function, a highly complicated system of cross-referencing takes place between them. To state this activity in the simplest possible terms, the lobes act in stereo. And it must be firmly stated that the *outward* activity exhibited by the lobes as a twin function is that of the conscious mind. Both lobes still require the 'current' of pure consciousness to drive them.

In the everyday operation of the conscious mind, most of the motor activity is at the direction of the left hand lobe, with certain special qualities supplied by the right, the whole mix constituting that which is perceived to be the subject's personality. However, in the event of psychic trance being induced in the subject, the right hand lobe will become more active, and if given free rein, will create alternative personalities and situations, the scope of which is only limited by the subject's belief in them. But this state, I make it clear, is no pathway to the pure consciousness.

The Attention

The agent, or instrument, by which the pure consciousness (the subconscious mind) operates in the external world is known to us as the Attention. In the act of turning our whole attention upon a given object, we focus the power of the subconscious for reception by way of the five senses, and everything that the attention comprehends is indelibly recorded on the sphere of the subconscious. This act of recording is not to be confused with the Memory, that part of the conscious mind which retains impressions that seem uppermost at the time. Unlike the memory, which is fallible, the subconscious records everything – but when memory fails us, we are not able to call upon the subconscious to help unless a definite link exists between the two minds. Normally, this link does not exist to the extent at which a conscious mind can benefit from it at will.

As we have already determined, the necessary link cannot be forged unless subjugation and control of the thought-stream is achieved. As to how this may be accomplished, some small hint may be gleaned by the observation of ordinary, everyday circumstances. For example, in the watching of a television play, the necessary but possibly mundane events leading up to a moment of high drama may capture only part of our interest, allowing other thoughts and conversations to take place at the same time. But at moments of peak drama or horror, the attention becomes transfixed on the screen, discursive thought and conversation ceasing while we sit spellbound. During these critical few moments, the act of speculative thought ceases entirely and the *whole attention* is concentrated upon one point alone, a fact which is scarcely noticed by the subject, for as soon as the moment has passed, the mind immediately reverts, the thought-stream resuming its incessant activity. The all important point, un-noticed by the subject, is that the thought-stream can be temporarily halted by concentrating the attention fixedly upon one single objective. In the above example, the phenomenon is dependent upon the external attraction of the television programme, the transmission of which, so far as the ordinary viewer is concerned, is largely a matter of chance. To forge the link between the conscious and the subconscious it is necessary to create the same suspension of thought at will by turning the attention upon the subconscious itself, inward to that strange television screen at the back of the mind, and inducing the same state of rapt interest. Here the greatest difficulty lies, for the meditator is required to concentrate on what will for a long time appear to be, apart from random 'memory' images, absolutely nothing at all.

The Understanding

Whilst the attributes of the conscious mind – thought, emotion, memory, imagination – are familiar forces in our waking world, those of the subconscious remain barely comprehended. As an instance, we may consider the difference between 'knowledge' and 'understanding', two nouns with an interpretation so close that they are often wrongly assumed to be interchangeable. Yet there is a gulf of difference in their true meaning. Knowledge is an attribute of the conscious mind, a product of our memory. Understanding, on the other hand, is an intuitive force which stems only from the subconscious. To further analyse, we hold up the work of Sir Isaac Newton as an example of how understanding is gained. When Newton began his long study of gravitation he had only current knowledge in his memory with which to work. By long concentration, however, he was able to arrive at a point when his mind delivered to him knowledge not previously contained in the memory, but which allowed him to formulate his famous theory. During the course of his study he acquired a great deal of knowledge concerning relative subjects, but still without the revelation later experienced. At the completion of his work, however, he at last *understood* the principles for which he had been searching. But exactly where did this understanding come from, and why was it conveyed to Newton alone when others had approached the subject only to come away empty handed? The answer is that prolonged concentration by Newton on one single idea, or quest, sustained over a great period of time, had wrested from the subconscious a spark of *intuition* which induced understanding of hitherto unrealised possibilities. Once such an intuitive idea had been 'proved' by material calculation, the understanding then moved into memory to become knowledge.

If Newton's experience is compared with those of other great contributors to the world's knowledge, the ultimate conclusion can only be that the subconscious is a vast storehouse of wisdom, a storehouse that can only be unlocked and tapped by those who make the necessary effort to find the mental key.

Conscience and Immortality

Since the faculty of Intuition lies beyond the sense of reason, there is no adequate way in which it can be described, except perhaps as a vague feeling of 'knowing' without knowing why. The same may be said for that quality we name conscience, the invisible monitor of our moral behaviour. Nowhere is the effect of conscience more expressively revealed than in the child who tells a lie and then blushes uncontrollably. Later in life, many learn to overcome and ignore the inner voice: an unfortunate choice of conduct, for while they continue to do so they quite effectively bar their own approach to the realm of the subconscious and can therefore never fully partake of the benefits on offer. It is strange that so few people ever attempt to find out why conscience is there in the first place.

Another elusive quality of the subconscious is that of immortality, the concept of which is consistently misinterpreted.

We hear much of immortality in legend and myth; even more from the realm of modern fiction where the plot contrives either a super-human being or an indestructible body. But the simple truth is that while real immortality will never be available as an asset of the physical body, it most certainly is carried in the human mind, and to detect it, only a little self-analysis is required. Our outward self, the personality motivated by the conscious mind, registers time during the course of life by way of the passing seasons and the growth and ageing of the physical body. Diminishing motor responses as the years go by, along with a drastic change in physical appearance, constitutes the universal conception of 'old age', but if this habitual conception can be temporarily set aside, with analysis concentrated upon the impersonal Self within, it will be realised that this Self, the real 'I', looks out on the world in a manner no different at seventy years of age than at seven. This impersonal, ageless seat of observation is alone the immortality depicted in myth – and it can be reached, but not until the conscious mind has undergone the necessary development. I add that such development has been given legendary names that will not be unfamiliar to you – the Elixir of Life and the Fountain of Youth.

The allegorical writers were only too well aware that this development was achieved by a process which consisted of turning the conscious mind inward, focussing attention upon the subconscious in a form of mental feedback. At face value, this would appear to be a pointless exercise, but it must not be forgotten that the agent of the subconscious, the attention, operates through the medium of the waking, conscious mind, a lower intelligence compared to the former. By turning the attention inward upon itself, the subconscious that is normally in deep concealment is slowly drawn out, gradually to permeate the conscious mind with a higher *understanding*. Thus, in a growing process, the elevated conscious mind becomes aware of even greater possibilities and the method by which they may be turned into realities.

It is vital for the reader to comprehend that the extent of these mysterious benefits are never over-emphasised, no matter how glowing are the terms used to describe them. Real power of a very special nature is made available to the successful adept of the mental work. If this were not so, there would hardly be any logical reason for writer after writer, down through the centuries, to indulge each in his own carefully constructed contribution to the grand allegorical library.

> '. . . next to the soul,' they have stated. 'It is the most beautiful and precious thing on earth, and has the power to pull down kings and princes. . . '

True Religion

So great and uncompromising are these natural powers that they are recognisable as the very foundation of human life itself, and thus constitute the true basis of all religion. Much error prevails in the religious world, for virtually all external religions – Christianity, Mohammedism, Buddhism and the rest – are practised by faithful adherance to the guidelines laid down in their respective Bibles. Unfortunately, almost all such conformists are unaware that much of their sacred texts are allegorical and are not meant to be read so literally. The only true illuminative statements about religion will be found in the writings of those few who have achieved the higher level of *understanding* – the adepts of the process. To draw upon a single one, we may examine the idea set out by the noted 19th century Rosicrucian, Franz Hartmann.

To begin with, Hartmann states, Man operates through the conscious mind alone. For all his supposed intelligence, he is no more than an animal, conscious only of his bodily desires and elementary instincts. He has no conception of the divine element within, the subconscious, that which we call God. One day, however, he experiences a presentiment of something spiritually higher. Casually interested, he begins to seek for this higher element, although continuing to be dominated by his lower, animal mind. Gradually, the desire to find it grows stronger until it counter-balances his lower nature. At times, he searches diligently for the higher element, at others he returns to the lower mode of life. Later, increasingly anxious, he actively institutes a search for the mysterious and elusive higher element, but as his quest is conducted externally, he is unable to find it. Towards the end of his quest, he discovers the higher element within himself and his spiritual senses are awakened enough so that he may recognise others at the same level. Finally, he discovers the greatest truth of all, that *he himself* is the God for which he has been seeking. His will is now free from every selfish desire, his thoughts are under the complete control of his will, and his *Word* (i.e., his ideas) becomes a *creative act*.

Franz Hartmann concludes by stating:

> Such a spiritual being may still dwell in a human body upon this planet and not even be recognised as something superior to the rest of mankind; for his personality is not God. He lives and yet he lives not; for it is God, his divine Self, the eternal Reality living in him.

To put this in modern parlance, we may say that by means of the contemplative process, the subconscious mind of the adept becomes dominant over the conscious mind. This transcendence, however, is purely mental, a development of *understanding*, something that cannot normally be detected externally. It does not mean that the adept concerned will be subject to religious visions, or the hearing of strange voices which he thinks are the words of God. When the old philosophical texts describe the seeing of a 'light in the dark of the mind', they do not necessarily mean the internal seeing of a flash of brilliance. The 'illumination' in most cases referred to is an enhanced sense of understanding, which may develop slowly, or alternatively, may arrive suddenly in the form of a revelation.

At its ultimate, this development allows the adept to comprehend the mystery of Creation and the part which Man plays in it, but here we encounter that which the 20th century likes to call a Catch 22 situation. The further along the path of understanding the adept travels, the harder it becomes for him to convey in mere words that which he has begun to comprehend. Thus it will appear to those left behind that the adept is being deliberately secretive, when in fact the fault lies with the inadequacy of words to describe certain states. To transmit to readers, for instance, the concept of Relativity as proposed by Albert Einstein, writers must necessarily resort to analogous devices related to the material world. This is only partly successful, for many who read about the theory are still unable to grasp the concept in its entirety because their understanding is yet at only an average level. The explanation of Relativity is a part of the mystery of Creation and those who can understand it are on the first steps of a ladder leading to the highest wisdom – the 'wisdom' which the philosophical texts describe as the 'inexpressible Word of God'.

I pause here to point out that this book is dedicated in style and form to all those with a normal level of understanding, confining the expositions of allegory to a language that should be readily comprehensible by all. For those readers who would prefer an alternative analysis of the pure consciousness and its effect upon those in whom it has manifested, I suggest the now classic volume, *Cosmic Consciousness* by Richard M. Bucke (E.P. Dutton USA 1969). Although the author, who has experienced a form of enlightenment personally, does not deal in allegory, his text gives valuable insight into the mystery of the inner mind and the necessary development of moral integrity.

The Mental Work

It is purely due to the factor of developed *understanding* that the allegorical language can exist, for the whole system depends upon the interchanged meanings of words and phrases, the relationship of which can only be fully comprehended when the sense of intuition begins to grow. To complicate matters even more, it will be shown that although there are well-worn guide lines to the system, set down by those in earlier times, each adept writer did not hesitate to bring his own creative ability into play in order to express the main theme in a manner personal to himself. Each set an individual seal on his personal contribution to the catalogue. It is no wonder that the great mass of ordinary people have remained unaware, either of the hidden theme which the allegory expresses, or that the texts concerned contained an allegory at all. Who, for instance, would suspect that Rider Haggard's famous romance, *She*, is a vehicle for the concealed message? Or that the same allegorical form has now found its way into modern film scripts?

Quite obviously this book cannot provide a precise key by which the reader may gain immediate and total insight to all allegorical texts, but by means of example – some revelatory – it may persuade the sceptic that there is indeed a message of great import to be unearthed, or at least that there is some special knowledge that he has previously been unable to detect, but it can go no further than that. The rest of the work is the responsibility of the reader alone who, by his own efforts, must endeavour to expand his power of understanding until at last the *veil of the temple is rent*.

The outline of the mental process which follows is brief and will hardly constitute a satisfactory explanation for those who are keen to discover how it should be undertaken. But this volume is devoted to an exposition of the allegorical code rather than to the provision of a full key to the mental work, although it may be said that, after assimilation of the allegorical texts and the subsequent realisation of their scope, the reader will be ready to approach the subject of the process in a far more prepared state of mind.

The Hermetic process has something of a parallel in Isaac Newton's quest into the mysteries of gravitation, for it is a fact of life that if specific knowledge is required, the seeker must bend his concentration to it with unceasing zeal. Newton achieved this in magnificent style, so lost at times in his mental cogitations that he completely forgot his meals. It took him many years, but in the end his understanding of gravitation allowed him to set down his *Principia*, unquestionably a major contribution to the advancement of scientific knowledge at the time. In the same fashion, the inner mental growth requires sustained effort over a definite period of time. For most seekers, the process will take some years to complete, unless a revelatory experience intervenes.

Following the pattern laid down by Franz Hartmann, let us

now set out a guide to the whole course of the mental work. It can be outlined in seven stages;

1   At the outset, the aspirant-to-be is in complete ignorance of his own subconscious powers, although in material life he may be financially secure and therefore relatively content.

2   There may come a time in his life, however, when in spite of his worldly achievements, he becomes conscious of a vague dissatisfaction with life. He feels an inner yearning for something more, but has no idea what it could be.

3   At odd times, he may begin to wonder at the purpose of life, or to question his conception of religion and God. A vague doubt enters his mind.

4   Uneasy, he devotes his spare time to a casual research of the subjects he has so far ignored and which he has previously considered unimportant; God, spiritual powers, and the paranormal in general. Soon he finds a whole new world of strange myth and unexplained phenomena, and is introduced to the idea that Man has spiritual powers but does not know how to apply them. However, he only half believes such stories, for many have been proved to be false, and in any case, they are at odds with his logical reasoning.

5   After some time, his increasing desire to know the truth, and his suspicions that his logic may after all be at fault, urge him to engage in more active and dedicated research. He reads to increase his knowledge of the related subjects. Perhaps he investigates the outward forms of magic and parapsychology at first hand. At times he is confident that such a spiritual power does exist. At others, his sense of reason asserts itself and scepticism prevails.

6   Years of enquiry may pass before his understanding is sufficiently developed to allow him knowledge of a spiritual power secreted in his own mind. Gradually, certain directives, hitherto completely misunderstood, lead him to differentiate between the two aspects of the mind – the conscious and the subconscious. The power, he realises, is in the subconscious, but to reach it he needs to gain full control of his outer thoughts and emotions. For

the first time he understands *why* it is said that thought can be a creative force. He begins a daily period of meditation. After a great deal of study, he is able to read the allegorical code that is everywhere around him, and is led to the further realisation that his previous doubts and ingrained scepticism have been the stumbling block to his progress. He sweeps them away. But to do this effectively, requires a great internal struggle. He must set himself *mentally* apart from his friends and acquaintances who still inhabit the world to which his personality has so far belonged. The personality itself, he is forced to understand, is the wrong vehicle for the kind of progress he now desires, and the importance he attaches to it must be, by an act of will power, diminished until it is finally killed off altogether. It is not an easy thing to do, for it demands of him a tremendous psychological change. Quite often he is tempted to revert to his old way of thinking and living.

7   If he is one of the fortunate few – the *blessed* – he at last develops an understanding which shows him how to control his mind, and by doing so, reaches the pure consciousness within. Once there, he will know how to use it as a creative force. He has at his disposal the greatest force in Nature.

Chapter Two

The Allegorical Pattern

Certain academics, although unable to penetrate to the core of the allegorical theme as it has been outlined, have nevertheless noticed the presence of a pattern, an almost predictable sequence in the construction of mythological stories, notwithstanding the fact that centuries of time may separate each from the other. This pattern can be briefly outlined as follows:

1. Supernatural origin of the hero; generally a miraculous birth accompanied by notable portents, such as a flash of lightning, a thunderbolt, or an earthquake.
2. Perils menacing the hero's infancy, with a fortuitous escape from evil or death.
3. A form of initiation into a secret wisdom, or the discovery of a strange and ancient book.
4. Travel over land and sea in search of more wisdom, a quest which is long, arduous and beset with dangers.
5. A magical contest; a temptation scene; a combat.
6. A trial, or a persecution.
7. A sacrifice, or a mysterious death.
8. A resurrection to immortality, or the discovery of a great hoard of treasure in an unknown land.

No doubt, even a casual glance at this sequence will strike a familiar chord, but it must be firmly held in mind that all these events are sheer fiction, and that they have been specially collated in this style so as to express, in allegorical form, the mental process previously described. To relate the myth to the real circumstances we align the fiction with steps six and seven of the preceding list and reinterpret them thus:

1. The supernatural origin of the hero, such as a virgin birth,

along with the shock effects of the various portents are meant to portray the sense of revelation at the discovery of a spiritual power in man's own mind. The 'hero', of course, is the would-be adept as he pursues the course of his quest.

2 But doubt and scepticism still pervade his mind. If the aspirant is lucky, he may avoid being overwhelmed by negative thoughts.

3 Concentration upon the subject, combined with the practice of meditation slowly develops the faculty of understanding, and intuitively the aspirant feels compelled to continue; that his goal is not a figment of his imagination.

4 For a long time, possibly years, the aspirant seeks for the inner goal. It requires great stamina and patience.

5 Often he will be tempted to give up and return to his old way of thinking.

6 If he attempts to discuss his new ideas with others not of the same point of view, he will become the subject of ridicule. As the understanding develops, he is subject to even more radical change in outlook, and is forced to keep his thoughts to himself, or to seek out new friends of the same mind.

7 The peak of upheaval is reached when he realises that the importance normally placed on the preservation of his ego, the personality, must be forsaken if he is to proceed. This 'sacrifice', or 'death' can only be achieved when the understanding has reached a critical stage in its development. And if the aspirant succeeds, then the way is open to the final stage.

The last phase of the mythological pattern corresponds to step seven in the preceding list. If fortunate, the aspirant discovers how to control his mind and his emotions, and by doing so, gains access to the great powers which Nature affords. Thus, there is 'resurrected' an entirely new mentality from the remnants of the old – and with Nature's powers at his disposal, the initiate has found the 'buried treasure'.

How easy it would be to interpret the old myths if the pattern so outlined represented the sum total of the allegorical code. Unfortunately, it is no more than a bare framework upon which is fabricated a bewildering network of symbolic words and phrases, each with a deeply buried meaning comprehensible only to the initiated. Interpretation of some rely on no more than a phonetic equivalent, or an anagrammatical rearrangement of letters. For others, decipherment is almost a lost art, for the origins may lie in languages now dead, leaving what remains as a veritable trip wire to those endeavouring to pick their way through to the truth.

The range and scope of this vast collection of symbols is such that any attempt to present them all would be futile. Therefore, I give some preliminary examples now, leaving others to be defined as they appear in the various expositions. Selected at random, this list may stem in origin from 5,000 B.C. to the present day, and each code word is significantly emphasised in the same manner in which it will be presented in the expositions to come.

The Pure Consciousness

As this is the ultimate goal in which resides the great powers of Nature, it has always been represented by anything that is *good*, of the highest quality, of great mystery and strength, or as the saviour of mankind. It has been called: *purity*; *happiness*; a *friend*; a *companion*, or *brother*; a *garden*, or a *forest*; the colour and the metal *gold*; a *treasure*, a *diamond*, or a *pearl of great price*; one of high birth such as a *king*, a *prince*, or a *nobleman*; a *perfect* state like that proposed by Plato; a *temple*, or a *holy city*; a *lost city* or a *ruined city*; an *oasis*; a mythical, faraway land, long lost but still awaiting rediscovery, like *Eden*, *Atlantis*, *Shamballah*, or *Avalon*; a *lion*, because it is the king of beasts; by the zodiacal sign of *Leo*; a *star* by the ancient Egyptians because they considered stars to be the nearest thing to permanency and therefore representative of *immortality*.

In external religions it has been personified by the names *Osiris*, *Brahma*, *Ormazd*, *Zeus*, *Allah*, *Jehovah* and *God*, to mention only a meagre few. But the principle symbol by which the pure consciousness has always been depicted is the SUN, because as the physical orb is the centre of our universe, so the pure consciousness is at the *centre* of our mind.

The Conscious Mind

Because the incessant thought-stream, generated while in the waking state, effectively bars access to the pure consciousness and its beneficience, the conscious mind has been symbolised by anything that represents *evil* or *ugliness*. In a well known nursery tale the pure consciousness is hidden beneath the guise of *beauty*, whilst the conscious mind is the *beast*. Elsewhere, in folklore, myth, or even dramatic and romantic fiction, it is portrayed as a *toad*; a *monster*; a frightful *giant*, or any character that is misshapen or deformed. Because the conscious mind is the lower, animal part of the would-be initiate, it is naturally portrayed as an animal, such as a *dog*, perhaps because of its incessant and *noisy* bark, or a *pig*, because it is an *ugly* animal that loves to wallow in *dirt and dung* (the conscious mind loves to stay in its unpurified state), or a *horse*, an *ass*, or a *mule*. The Hindu religion characterises the conscious mind with its incessant thought-stream as a *mad monkey*. The ancient Egyptians on the other hand, preferred to use that ugly monster, the Nile *crocodile*. Two examples likely to be already familiar to readers are the *dragon* and the *serpent*, but perhaps the best known in modern times, although the general public is completely unaware of its significance, is the *vampire*, for the horrific tales in which Count Dracula plays his ghoulish part are based solely upon an allegorical representation of the mental process.

The Process

By far the greater mass of symbolism is devoted to the act of the process in all its stages, and we may begin at the point where the aspirant realises that he must turn his thoughts and concentration inward. As you will appreciate, this is a complete reversal of the normal direction in which the attention is attuned, and therefore it is characterised as such. Pictorially, it may be depicted as a man, or an animal, *looking back* over its own shoulder, or by something or someone placed, or *hanging upside down*. In texts you may find it referred to in the most innocuous manner with the mere mention of a 'going in another direction'. As a classic example of the mythical application we may cite the boatman of the Egyptian Mysteries, whose name was 'Face-behind', because it was *necessary for him to face backwards* so that he could pole the boat from the stern across the *Lily Lake* (act of reflection). The later Greek equivalent is more familiar as Charon. There is also the classic symbol of the snake which is depicted swallowing its own tail.

The act of reversing the attention in order to look in at the real 'I' is equivalent to gazing at oneself in a mirror. Consequently, it was called Reflection, although in many cases the term Meditation was substituted. As might be expected, it was symbolised in the allegorical tracts by the simple expedient of introducing into the storyline a *mirror*, a *lake*, or any other reflecting surface such as a polished shield. Perusal of the grand alchemical library will soon reveal that the most popular symbol of reflection by far was that great natural mirror, the *Moon*. But as repeated use of the lunar orb in this symbolic manner might constrict the imagination of the allegorical scribes, countless alternatives were employed, relating to the moon itself rather than to its power of reflection. Thus the inner meaning was cloaked in a double symbolism, for when the figures of, say, *Isis*, *Demeter*, *Diana*, or the *Virgin Mary* are examined for their root meanings, the researchers will ultimately arrive at the Moon and are likely to wrongly believe that penetration to the core of the symbolism has been achieved.

The place where the reflective act is put into practice, the inner mind, has been given many equally misleading names, among them a *vase*; *vessel*; *retort*; *ship*; *cave*; *coffin*; *tomb*; *casket*; *tree*; *mine*; *tower*; *furnace*; *laboratory*. It has often been depicted as a forlorn place, far away and removed from all normal channels of communication, like a *desert*; an uninhabited *island*; the far *North*; or the *Nether Regions*. The list is almost endless and we will become better acquainted with the rest as we proceed.

The two main forces instrumental in the process are the Attention, and the requisite amount of Concentration. In terms of allegory, it is difficult to separate this pair one from the other, for they go together, and as far as success in the process is concerned, one is totally useless without its companion. Perhaps we may loosely distinguish between them by saying that the Attention is often called *water*, while the Concentration is known as the secret *fire*. When these two qualities are combined in the correct manner in the course of the reflective act, it is then that the mind becomes the *vase*, or the *vessel*, whilst the two combined forces themselves are named *mercury*. This latter term, however, is merely the best known of literally hundreds of obscure titles, some of which are; *smoke*; *humidity*; *blood*; *woman*; *field*; *bath*; *vinegar*; *vitriol*; *sperm*; *mother*; *our water*; *argent-vive* (quicksilver); and most aptly on one occasion, *inspector of concealed things*.

The whole length of the mental work, although in itself a continuous act carried out by means of a daily period of meditation, was divided into three phases, and so the figure *three* is always strongly featured in allegorical texts. Each section was designated by a colour and these, it must be noted, follow a fixed progression.

The first colour is *black* and is intended to portray the long period from the beginning of the process up to the time when the thought processes begin to be dominated by the will of the operator. Such mastery over the unbridled forces of the mind is only obtained after a lengthy period of hard labour, during which the personality is 'softened' and gradually changed as enlightenment overtakes it. This subjugation has been dramatically described as a 'slow and agonising death', but of course, the 'death' referred to is not to be feared as a physical demise. It is more a clearing out of outmoded and erroneous ideas, leaving the psyche empty to take on a new and far superior personality. Thus the old masters describe this first stage with words designed to conjure up the idea of death, dissolution or subjugation. In many instances, allusion to the colour *black* would be outright, and a brief sample would be: *sacrifice*; *destruction*; *manure*; *black earth*; *melancholy*; *cloud*; *night*; *sublimated spirit*; *eclipse of the sun*; *shadows*; *raven* or *black bird*; *corruption*; *abyss*; *lead* (the metal); *Saturn*.

Alchemists of the Middle Ages, their allegorical jargon borrowed extensively from that of the chemist and the metallurgist, have called it *reduction*; *calcination*; *separation*; and *conjunction*. Alternatively, writers have symbolised it with certain forms of physical death, notably *hanging*, or *strangling*.

It is this first stage which requires so much patience and mental stamina from the would-be adept, and thus it has been depicted as a long *journey* through the *desert*, or the *wilderness*; as the climbing of a high *mountain*; as a *combat to the death*; as a *flagellation*, such as a boy whipping a top or simply as a man being flogged; or by any physical act which demands exertion and effort, as in a *man running*.

The second colour of the process is *white*, and designates the acquisition of mastery by will power over the incessant stream of thoughts. In the same fashion as before, the adept writers utilised any material connection with the colour white, or with the idea of purification, enlightenment, or approaching perfection. Thus, this second stage has been characterised by such names as; *white lamb*; *white copper*; *purified mercury*; *diamond* (because it is a *precious stone*, and white in colour); *limestone*; *lily*; *December* (because of the white snows); *virgin's milk*; *full moon*; *magnesia*; *salt of the metals*; *glass*; *white rock*.

Because at this point the adept holds within his grasp the instrument of the controlled mind with which he can easily complete the process, the white stage has at times been depicted as a flaming, or glittering *sword*, possibly with magical properties. In this respect there is the fabulous sword of King Arthur, Excalibur, which was embedded in a *stone*, or which was held up from the *water* of a *lake*.

The final stage of the process is signified by the colour *red*, and indicates complete mastery by the adept over his own mind, an achievement which bestows upon him the gifts of the subconscious. A random selection of names would include: *Adam*; *ruby*; *red rose*; *poppy*; *red stone*; *dawn*; *morning*; *red earth*; *blood*; *sulphur*; *red wine*; *gold*; *royal crown*; *celestial fire*; *red lion*.

Certain other colours were attached to this sequence, but they are employed less, and so will be described as and when we encounter them. For now, it may be noted that the colour *green* was indicative of initiation – that is, the acquisition of the knowledge which allows one to start the mental work in the correct manner. And because the man who chose to undergo the process dealt with these colours, he was often referred to as an *artist*.

The length of time taken to complete the process will differ according to the qualities of each individual aspirant and therefore no set period applicable to all can be stated. As one would expect, however, the allegorists made sure to depict set periods, none of which have any foundation in reality, but are merely code numbers, the presence of which will indicate that the process is being covertly referred to. Naturally, the number *three* is always heavily featured in this respect, indicating the three stages just discussed. Alternatively, the Egyptian and Sumerian hieroglyphics chose the number *fifty*, while in the biblical texts, *forty* and *seven* are most used. So well established did this latter pair become that later writers seldom attempted to replace them with newly invented alternatives, and you may confidently expect to encounter them within allegories penned as late as the beginning of the 20th century.

Another major symbol of the process in its entirety is that of a *ladder*, usually depicted with *nine* rungs, the biblical Ladder of Jacob being the most popular example. The figure nine symbolised the completion of the process and to give just a single instance of its application, note that Jesus *died on the cross* at the ninth hour (Matt. 27; 46).

It would be easy to continue filling many pages with the myriad of names applied to the various aspects of the mental work, but the only sure way in which to familiarise yourself with the Language of the Gods is to work with it, even if it is not fully comprehended at first. To demonstrate how the information so far given can serve as an initial guide, let us commence by applying it to the ancient story of Zoroaster, the great Persian prophet of pre-Christian times.

The Myth of Zoroaster

Originally named Zarathustra until Greek philosophers gave him his better known appellation, this personage was the figurehead of a religion extant in Persia from about 700 B.C. until 600 A.D. No one knows for certain if Zarathustra or Zoroaster was the real name of the man who originally introduced the religion into Persia, but perhaps you may form your own conclusion when I point out that 'Zoroaster' can mean 'son of a star', or *Son of the Sun*. The latter term was often used to designate an initiate of the mental process.

The Zoroastrian doctrine was a simple expression of Dualism comparable to, and indeed derived from, that expressed in the Indian Vedas – the concept of Light against Darkness, *good* versus *evil*. Mazdao (Ahura Mazda, or as he is later named, Ormazd), the God of Good, is a primaeval spirit who existed before the world began and although he wills good, his influence is restricted by his twin brother, Ahriman, the God of Evil. Man, the religion states, is a creation of Mazdao, who therefore has the right to call him to account. But Mazdao created Man free to determine his own actions, thus leaving him accessible to the influence of Ahriman, the Evil one. The remnants of this concept can be detected in our own religion, in the idea of Man with God at one hand and Satan on the other.

Those who are unable to comprehend the allegory in this statement regard the concept only as an expression of moral right and wrong with the material outcome determined by Man's cognisance of existing man-made laws. The initiated, however, know it to be symbolic of the two states of the human mind, the conscious mind being characterised as *evil*, the subconscious as *good*, for the reasons previously stated. The same allegory, but presented in a slightly more elaborate form, is contained in the prophet's mythical life story, the central theme of which has been carefully salvaged from texts composed – according to the scholars who have examined the fragments – anywhere between 1,500 B.C. and 900 B.C.

Zoroaster was the product of a miraculous event, a *virgin birth*. Equally miraculous portents accompanied the event, the most striking of which was the fact that the infant *laughed out loud when he saw the light of day*, whereas every other babe born into the world has wept. At Zoroaster's arrival, Ahriman was thrown into fear and rage, and tried every means in his power to destroy the infant, but to no avail, for Zoroaster *escaped*. Destined for greatness, he attained youthful manhood, one of the manuscripts informing us that:

> . . . there is manifested in him a *mind which is more capacious than the whole world*, and more exalted than any worldly possession, with an *understanding* whose strength is *perfectly* selected . . .

In preparation for his sacred mission to bring religion to Persia, Zoroaster began to observe a strict *silence* at the age of *seven*, spending a long period *alone in the wilderness*, where he lived in a *cave* on the peak of a *snowy white mountain*. He was *thirty* years of age when his first revelation came to him. In pursuance of his mission, he was sorely *tempted* by Ahriman, but did not succumb. Instead, he embarked upon *many years of wandering*, leading a life of struggle and *conflict*. Eventually, he managed to convert a *king*, who became a champion of the Zoroaster faith. A bitter *conflict* which took place at the royal court, required Zoroaster to answer *thirty-three* questions over a period of *three* days, a test that he passed successfully enough to win over the king. But almost immediately, the king's priests poisoned the royal mind against the prophet so that he was *condemned to death*. Divine intervention, however, saved Zoroaster, granting him *immortality* by means of

   . . . something that resembled *honey*.

To interpret the allegory within the framework of this quaint fable, two comparisons are required. The first must be made with the tabled pattern of events given at the beginning of this chapter. It will be seen that Zoroaster's story conforms in almost every respect and thus, by its plot alone, we are given the broadest of hints as to the real nature of the text. The second comparison must be made with the list of code words already discussed so as to check on the inner meanings of those words especially emphasised in the story. To demonstrate, I will now repeat the main events and interpret them as they occur.

The name Zoroaster itself (*Son of the Sun*) personifies an initiate of the process, someone who has actually embarked upon the mental work, and this is confirmed right at the outset when we are told that he was the product of a miraculous birth, that he was *born of a virgin* (is the product of the act of reflection). Zoroaster differed from all other infants at birth because he laughed out loud. This is an obscure hint. He laughed because he was *happy*, a code word frequently found in allegorical works and has the concealed meaning of 'initiated'. This shows us that the 'birth' alluded to was not a physical one, but the birth of his renewed personality.

At the infant's arrival, Ahriman tried hard to destroy him, but failed. At the beginning of the practice, it is extremely hard to control the thought-stream. Many believe it to be impossible and give up, but those destined to become accomplished initiates will somehow find the patience to continue until they overcome the Ahriman of their own conscious minds. As Zoroaster attains manhood (as the process develops), he acquires a mind which is 'more capacious than the whole world' (his *understanding* develops beyond the normal bounds). In preparation for his mission (the accomplishment of the process), he observes a strict *silence* (he silences, or controls the wayward thoughts, acquiring the 'quiet' of a mind which is focussed on one single idea alone). The period spent *alone in the wilderness* depicts the length of the process, as does the figure *seven* – while the *cave* is that dark recess where he does his meditation (the inner mind). The snowy *white* peak represents attainment of the second stage of the work, and the age of *thirty* (containing the figure *three*) indicates the stages in their entirety.

The trials and tribulations inflicted on Zoroaster at the *royal court*, (the mind in the course of the process) eventually resulted in his being condemned to *death* (the necessary 'death' of the conscious mind), a fate from which he was saved only by divine intervention and the subsequent granting of immortality (endeavouring to show that the 'death' in question does take place, but that it is of the utmost beneficence to the recipient).

The use of the term 'honey', otherwise known as *nectar*, signifies the power of reflection which aids in the development of the *understanding*. Just as the bee, little by little, gathers the material from which its honey is manufactured, so a daily period of meditation gathers the 'nectar' of pure consciousness. This analogy was popular with the ancient Egyptians and will, of course, be familiar to those who read the Bible texts.

I would like to emphasise the fact that the name 'Zarathustra' (or Zoroaster) does not refer to any specific person or sage who alone expounded the theory of Good versus Evil as laid out in the Persian documents. The name was simply a fictional shield behind which a small band of initiates could write and teach in anonymity. Seldom, if ever, did an initiate reveal his true name. If comparisons are required, a famous one arises in the name of Hermes Trismegistus, the Egypto-Greek initiate who supposedly wrote the Emerald Tablets. Students of alchemical literature will be aware that this name was no more than a cover for a number of writers, some of whom were from different time periods. And as the name Zoroaster is open to an interpretation relevant to the Hermetic process, so too is Hermes Trismegistus. *Hermes* is otherwise known as *Mercury* (the attention), and since the time of the Greek philosophers, all allegorical works of this nature have been referred to under the generic title 'Hermetic' (pertaining to *Mercury*). Trismegistus simply means 'thrice great', and quite obviously alludes to the three stages of the Great Work.

I draw this fact to the attention now because I have no doubt that discerning readers will have already marked the comparison between the mythical life of Zoroaster and that of Jesus Christ as recounted in the four Gospels, and wonder why. Another worthwhile comparison may be noted in the sage of Apollonius of Tyana, that *wise man* of magic and mystery. If examined carefully, the plot will be seen to adhere closely to the tabled pattern of events upon which allegories are concocted, drawing us to the obvious conclusion. As Madame Blavatsky pointed out:

> His visit to the empire of the wise men, and interview with their king, Hiarchas, the oracle of Amphiaraus, explain symbolically many of the secret dogmas of Hermes. They would disclose, if understood, some of the most important secrets of nature . . .
>
> (*Isis Unveiled*, Vol I, page 37)

As for the name itself, *Apollonius of Tyana*, the initiate author Fulcanelli, in his *Le Mystère des Cathédrales*, has suggested it to be a phonetic equivalent to the god names Apollo and Diana. To the initiated, these names represent the *Sun* (the subconscious) and the *Moon* (the reflective action of the conscious mind). Thus, if it is understood that there is no literal truth in the above-mentioned myths, that their figureheads never actually existed as real persons, and that the carefully devised plots did not necessarily depict events that took place in reality, but that they were manipulated so as to accommodate the allegory, then the reader will be receiving the first glimmerings of true *understanding*.

I am aware that it will be supremely difficult, if not impossible, for a devout Catholic to adjust to the fact that the Jesus of the Gospels never trod the dust of Jerusalem, that his name was specially coined, like those previously discussed, merely as a figurehead for use by the initiate who, in the first century A.D., carefully built the myth into its Gospel form, and that the sole object of the 'Testaments' was to project in allegorical style the way to the mental process. However, the weight of evidence yet to be presented may hopefully steer the doubtful towards, if not through, the gate to enlightenment.

Chapter Three

It is my intention, in later chapters, to present full length examples of allegorical works, along with the necessary interpretation, but the reader must be prepared to find that not every explanation will be readily comprehensible at first sight. It requires a little time to become adjusted to the vast network of Hermetic catch-phrases and code words. More especially it is necessary to set aside erroneous knowledge and accept that many historical 'facts' are not facts at all, but are allegorical fiction. The Gospels are a prime example, but there are many others of equal interest and importance. Bewildering also is the revelation that the material containing the allegories emanates from the most unexpected and diverse sources – from the Bible to biographies, from philosophy to fiction. The allegories can be short and simple, or long and heart-breakingly complicated; they can appear in works of the highest philosophical and theosophical merit, and also be detected in fairy tales.

The Tiger That Ate Grass

An example of the most basic type of allegory is to be found in Indian sacred literature where Ramakrishna tells the story of the tiger that gave birth to a cub just as it sprang on a flock of sheep. Unnoticed by its parent, the cub was left to grow up among the sheep, where it learnt to bleat like a lamb and eat grass for sustenance. One day, another tiger attacked the flock and was astonished to discover the strange tiger cub which bleated like a sheep. It grabbed the cub by the scruff of its neck, dragged it to a nearby pool and made it look at its own reflection. To make sure it fully understood, the tiger smeared blood on the cub's mouth, at which – with some hesitancy – the cub began to accept its true identity.

In this quaint tale, the cub characterises the ordinary human who lives with no knowledge of the superior strength and power within his mind. He remains in ignorance until such time as an inner prompting causes him to take up the practice of mental reflection (the cub is made to look at *himself* in the reflecting surface of the *water*), whereupon he gains access to his true Self, the subconscious (symbolised by the *blood*).

The Vampire

Another relatively straightforward allegory is that concealed within the more familiar legend of the blood-sucking vampire. You may be quite sure that this myth, with its modern cinematic treatment, portraying the evil Count Dracula's nightly excursions by the light of the full moon, has no foundation in reality. To demonstrate its allegorical content, we must examine the basic conditions necessary for the vampire's existence, as stipulated by the legend itself.

The vampire is a figure of the utmost *evil*, bound to his *grave* (same as *tomb*, or *coffin*), able to rise only at *night* when the *sun has gone down* and when the *moon* is full. Generally dressed all in *black*, he is quite frightful to look at – that is, he is *ugly*. Sometimes he assumes the form of a large, *ugly* bat, by which *transformation* he is able to fly abroad to seek out victims. When he traps one, he *drains the blood*, and in turn, they become as he is. The vampire can be repulsed by the *sign of the cross*, or by exposure to *sunlight*, but he can only be completely destroyed by a *stake driven through his heart*. Although empowered to mingle with humans without being recognised as a vampire, he can be detected by the fact that he *casts no reflection*, or shadow.

To arrive at the true meaning of all this legendary nonsense, it is only necessary to regard the 'vampire' as the conscious mind newly embarked on the mental work, hence it is dressed in *black*, and it is *ugly*. Its search for victims and the subsequent draining of their blood is in this instance intended to stylise the manner in which the conscious mind, in its use of the attention, daily draws upon the energy of the subconscious, but wastes it in wholly outward application, never returning such *blood* (pure consciousness – attention) in the practice of inward meditation. By setting this bad example, it incites others to follow suit, and so ignorance of the mental work is perpetuated. This is why the vampire is said to *cast no reflection* (does not meditate inwardly).

The vampire cannot operate in direct sunlight, meaning that the conscious mind remains bound in its coffin of ignorance as long as it fails to make contact with the *Sun*, the subconscious. The sign of the *cross*, by which means the vampire can be repulsed, is an age old symbol denoting the mental process and lastly, the *stake through the heart*, the only means by which the vampire may be 'killed', stands revealed as the process of meditation directed at the *heart* (centre) of the mind. Compare this with the legend of the Werewolf, a creature that must be killed with a *silver* bullet. The metal silver is always symbolically equivalent to the Moon, and therefore represents the act of reflection, by which the conscious mind (Werewolf) most certainly be 'killed'.

Virtually all allegories employ as a vehicle either a real event in history, or a natural phenomenon, the facts of which can be twisted, parodied or manipulated in order to accommodate the code phrases suitable to the initiate. In this case, the originator of the vampire legend worked his myth round the real animal, the vampire bat, which does indeed suck blood, is nocturnal, and is hardly very attractive to look at. But only the imagination of the conscious mind has elevated the myth to the level at which it is regarded today – as almost real!

The Camel and the Hump

As a most apt example of the single, Hermetic code word, I have selected *camel*, primarily because its application can be perceived over a great period of time, from the Old Testament era up to the beginning of the present century, and secondly, because it is so obscure, so far removed from the subject to which it really refers that unless a detailed explanation is provided, there is little or no chance of it registering in the reader's consciousness in his pursuance of the truth.

At its most superficial, the sign of the camel is analogous to the mental process because it is an animal that is used to *cross the desert* (complete the process), and because desert lore has it that the animal can travel for *three* days without water. Deeper investigation will show that a far larger part in the analogy is played by word association, phonetic equivalents in Aramaic, Hebrew and Greek which stem from a time when the written languages consisted of consonants only, the necessary vowels being left to the reader to insert according to interpretation of the textual subject. Familiar as we are with our present day system, where as little as possible is left to chance misinterpretation, it may not at first be clear how easy it was for the ancient writers to encode their message, or by what devious route this particular encipherment came into existence.

As a mere framework of an example, we may consider the letters G M L. By the insertion of two vowels to render 'Gimel', we have the third letter of the Hebrew alphabet, denoted in numerical terms by the figure three. As I have endeavoured to show, this number is prominent in Hermetic manuscripts as a symbol of the process, and so with this fact borne in mind, we now return to the 'camel'. By a substitution of vowels we quickly arrive at 'Gamal', the Hebrew word for 'camel'. By inference, therefore, however nebulous it may appear to you, the word for 'camel' is connected with the figure three, thus hinting at a possible connection with the mental work.

Another shift of vowels will render 'Gamul', meaning 'weaned', nothing to do with Hermeticism, you may think, until it is recalled that in the parlance of the allegorist, the newly born (or reborn) personality, is referred to as a *child*, or an *infant*. Thus 'Gamul' could easily represent that same child at a further stage of the mental process.

This type of word association was hinted at by the first century historian, Josephus, in *The Jewish Wars*, a text which contains much allegory. Describing a certain locale named Gamala, he explains that one flank of a mountain in the vicinity is prominent due to a ridge, the shape of which resembles the hump of a camel:

> Whence it derives its name, the natives pronouncing the sharp sound inaccurately . . .

By this, Josephus means that the first letter of the word 'camel' was spoken gutturally, resulting in 'gamel', hence Gamala, and on its own, this morsel of inconsequential information has no real inner significance. But with word association in mind, we note that 'Gamel' can also mean 'work', thus presenting the hidden hint of *work on oneself* – the mental work.

Such word association was to be found in other languages – sometimes interchangable with the original. The Greek word for 'camel' is 'Kamelos', and its near equivalent is 'Kamilat', meaning 'contemplation'. So well known among Hermetic writers was this particular example that later factions used it as a basis for the myth of King Arthur and *Camelot*. Yes, the Arthurian legends have Hermetic significance if one knows how to detect it.

In *The Sacred Mushroom and the Cross*, author John Allegro reveals much concerning the ancient art of punning and word play, and points out that another word for 'camel' is 'kirkarah'. This happens to be a close phonetic equivalent of 'kirkaia', the *Mandrake* plant. As I shall later show, the Mandrake was yet another code word employed by the initiate writers, it having virtually the same inner significance as that of 'camel', i.e. *essence*, the pure consciousness.

Many examples of *camel* in its role as a code word can be found in the Old and New Testaments, outwardly innocuous, the inner import of it completely overlooked by the general run of scholar. But before we proceed to examine them, it must be strongly stated that the supposedly divine writings of the Bible are nothing less than a compendium of Hermetic myths, each bearing the same concealed message as that of the Vampire, or of the Tiger that Ate Grass. The well known figures therein are personifications of the initiate only, and had no existence in real life, or if they had, their real existence bore no resemblance to that depicted in the scriptural stories. I am aware that this further undermining of established foundations of Christian belief will be deplored by many devout theologians, but if my word alone is of little worth, there are others who have penned the same truth and whose statements may command more respect. One such is the previously mentioned Rosicrucian, Franz Hartmann. In a long paragraph about the biblical patriarchs, he openly declared the stories of the Bible to be not real histories but

> . . . allegories and myths having always a deep meaning, of which our expounders of the Bible, as well as its critics, usually know very little. The men and women of the old and new 'testaments' are much more than mere persons supposed to have existed at the time. They are personifications of eternally active spiritual forces . . .
>
> (*Magic – Black and White*, page 33)

A random choice of Old Testament myth in which the *camel* code word plays its part might be the opening verses of the Book of Job.

1   There was a man in the land of Uz, whose name was Job; and that man was *perfect* and upright, and one that feared God and *eschewed evil*.
2   And there were born unto him *seven* sons and *three* daughters.
3   His substance also was *seven* thousand sheep, and *three* thousand *camels*, and five hundred yoke of oxen, and five hundred she asses, and a very great household; so that this man was the greatest of all the *men in the east*.

At ordinary appraisal, that is without the benefit of the emphasis I have placed on certain words and phrases, these verses are merely an outward expression of a character who, by the material standards of that era, is suitably well off. And so it is generally read. But the informed reader will take immediate note of the words I have indicated and place a very different interpretation on the verses. The first emphasised word 'perfect', is a code sign which represents the man who has accomplished the mental process. Thus, right from the very start we are told that Job is the personification of an initiate. This message is reiterated in the phrase telling us that he 'eschewed evil' (he no longer existed in the conscious mind but has made the transmission to the subconscious). This transmission can only be made by submitting oneself to the mental process; and we are reminded of this by the repeated use of the figures *seven* and *three*, both indicative of the length of the work. Another reference to Job as an accomplished initiate is made in the finale phrase, 'men in the east', for the *east*, you must remember, is where the *sun rises* (enlightenment dawns). To make this interpretation complete, I would add that a similar inner meaning is contained in the figure five hundred, but this is obscure and will take up more space than its importance warrants. I believe that what I have given is sufficient for the moment, although perhaps the way in which the Book of Job is concluded deserves clarification. In chapter 42, verse 12, the reader is told that Job has increased his total of camels to six thousand, and it may be felt that this statement negates the significance of the figure three formerly used. This is not so because the significant statement – the first use of the code number *three* – has already been made, effectively establishing the hidden message, and thus the figure six in the final chapter has no other duty than to tell us that, as an initiate, Job's blessings were doubled.

A second example is to be found in II Kings, chapter 8, verse 9, when Elisha (again personification of an initiate) comes to Damascus. Hearing of his arrival, the sick king, Ben Hadad, sends him *forty camels* bearing gifts.

In the New Testament, the *camel* emblem best open to interpretation is that in Matthew, chapter 3, verse 4. It concerns John the Baptist, a character who, so the text of Luke 1 tells us, was *born of a virgin*, and is therefore once again to be regarded as the personification of an initiate. In Matthew 3, it is said:

4   And the same John had his raiment of camel's hair . . .

In other words, just in case you missed the code phrase, *born of a virgin*, the camel hair coat tells us that John is clothed in the essence of the pure consciousness: he has accomplished the mental work.

A final aspect of the *camel* symbolism, and one which appeared strongly in later times, is that relating to the outward appearance of the animal. To the early Jews the camel was unclean and no one could deny that it was the ugliest of beasts, facts which the allegorical writers seized upon to portray it in a reversed role, as the conscious mind. In later times, the camel's hump became the focus of allegorical attention, transferring to the back of an ugly or deformed man, as in Victor Hugo's *The Hunchback of Notre Dame*. At the appropriate juncture we will examine the abundance of initiate code words worked into the text and the plot of this story, showing Hugo to be a master of allegorical writing.

There exists the probability that the 'hunchback' emblem was called upon long before the time of Hugo, and applied in an effort to counter historical propaganda. It is common knowledge that certain writers have called Richard the Third by the name 'crookback'. Yet portraits of this much maligned king show no sign of such a deformity. This mystery, too, will be examined in due course.

The Pearl of Great Price

Arabian and New Testament writers are two factions that made use of the pearl as a fitting symbol of the mental process. The pearl itself is a precious growth rather than a gemstone, and the way in which Nature manufactures it corresponds closely to the way in which the mental work takes place. A tiny grain of sand insinuates itself into the soft skin of the oyster, causing a substance to be built around it, just as a single thought will 'harden' in the mind if enough concentration is brought to bear. The substance develops at last into a much valued commodity, as does the single thought which will accomplish the process. Pearls take several years to form, just as the process takes several years to complete. There are other similarities between the two in that the pearl is milky *white* in colour; the oyster which is its mother is found in the *sea* (the sea of thought in the mind); and is most likely to be found in warm waters, therefore being seen as a *treasure* that will be produced under conditions of *gentle heat* (meditation).

The analogy is used sparingly in the Gospels and the two examples I give both come from the text of Matthew. First, in chapter 7, Jesus (personification of the initiate) is made to say:

6   Give not *that which is holy* unto the dogs, neither *cast your pearls before swine*, lest they trample them under their feet and turn again and rend you.

The admonition within this verse, repeated in two different ways, is for those who have achieved some success in the mental work to refrain from attempting to instruct any uninitiated person unless they are sure the aspirants have reached a desirable level of understanding. Give not that which is holy (the knowledge) to the *dogs* (symbol of the uninitiated conscious mind). Do not cast your pearls (knowledge) before swine (the *pig*, another symbol of the uninitiated conscious mind). If this warning is ignored, the knowledge may be misused (trampled underfoot), or the would-be teacher derided and persecuted (they will turn again, – i.e., return to the normal uninformed way of thinking – and rend you).

A better example of the pearl emblem can be found in Matthew 13, where Jesus is preaching to his disciples, explaining the *kingdom of heaven* (the completed process) by means of parables:

45   Again, the kingdom of heaven is like unto a merchant
      man, seeking goodly pearls.
46   Who, when he had found one pearl of great price, went
      and sold all that he had, and bought it.

The *pearl of great price*, likened to the *kingdom of heaven*, is the art
of the process, and the instruction is that to obtain it, one must
turn the attention away from its constant preoccupation with
things external (sell all one has) and concentrate instead upon the
inner mind.

There has been some conjecture that the pearl and oyster
symbolism was directly instrumental in the production of
Jonathan Swift's most famous work of allegory and satire,
Gulliver's Travels. The chemist, Robert Boyle, one of the great
17th century minds familiar with Hermetic allegory, wrote an
essay entitled 'Upon the Eating of Oysters'. Hermetic content
was there for those who could read it, but there also occurred the
following passage in a dialogue between the characters
Lindamore and Eugenius. Lindamore is discoursing on how
savage Indians will eat all manner of live animals and insects, just
as Eugenius is himself eating an oyster, excrement and all:

> 'You put me in mind of a fancy of your friend Mr Boyle',
> Eugenius replies. 'Who was saying that he had thoughts of
> making a short romantick story where the scene should be
> laid in some island in the southern ocean, governed by some
> rational laws and customs as those of *Utopia*, or the *New
> Atlantis*; and in this country he would introduce an
> observing native that, upon his return home from his
> travels made in Europe, should give an account of our
> countries and manners, under feigned names, and fre-
> quently intimate in his relations (or in his answers to
> questions that shall be made him) the reason of his
> wondering to find our customs so extravagant and differing
> from those of his country. For your friend imagined that by
> such a way of proposing many of our practices we should
> ourselves be brought unaware to condemn, or perhaps
> laugh at them, and should at least cease to wonder to find
> other nations think them as extravagant as we think the
> manners of the Dutch and Spaniards, as they are represented
> in our travel books'.

'I dislike not the project', says Lindamore. 'And I wish it were prosecuted by somebody that, being impartial, were more a friend to fables'.

To make clear the inner ramifications of this passage, it must be recognised that both works mentioned in the dialogue, Sir Thomas More's *Utopia*, and Sir Francis Bacon's *New Atlantis*, are texts which contain Hermetic allegory, thus showing that both authors were no strangers to the subject. Robert Boyle himself, in the latter period of his life, belonged to a small and exclusive circle of individuals who called themselves the 'Invisible College', each member of which possessed the same Hermetic knowledge. One prominent member contemporary to Boyle was Sir Isaac Newton. Another, although of a slightly later period, was Jonathan Swift.

To all the 'Invisibles', the discussion in Boyle's essay about oysters would inevitably relate to the symbol of the *pearl*, at once informing them that allegory was present and that the text should not be read wholly literally. By mention of the two Hermetic works, and with the words of the last sentence of dialogue, Boyle is expressing the wish for some writer of allegory other than himself to concoct a new vehicle for transmission of the concealed message. Thirty five years or so later, Jonathan Swift obliged.

Before Your Very Eyes

The special phrases employed by the allegorists are so numerous and diverse that to list them all would require a catalogue of considerable size, to say nothing of the time and effort necessary for its compilation. In a work of average length such as this, it is possible only to touch on selected items, and therefore the rest of this chapter will be devoted to those which have the most relevance to the major exposition to follow – phrases which, while likely to appear of no significance to the ordinary reader, would immediately catch the eye of those conversant with the code. My first example, a phrase employed as long ago as Old Testament times, is 'before your very eyes'.

Today only recognisable as the catchphrase of magicians and

illusionists the world over, uttered as they prepare to deceive
your eyes with the quickness of their hands, these few words
were originally used to indicate a more potent kind of magic.
They are to be found written into the allegorical story of Moses
and the *forty* year trek through the *wilderness* by the *Israelites* at a
time when that mysterious food, *Manna*, made its first
appearance. In my book *Hermes Unveiled* I have set down in some
detail the reasons why 'manna' was never a real phenomenon, it
being in reality a code word to symbolise, like the previously
mentioned *nectar*, the pure consciousness as it is gathered in the
act of meditation. For 'manna', therefore, read 'meditation' and
the developing understanding that results from it. If this
interpretation is accepted the nebulous connection with the code
phrase under discussion can be made clear.

In Numbers, chapter 11, the Israelites complain bitterly to
Moses about the lack of proper food:

4 And the mixt multitude that was among them fell a lusting;
   and the children of Israel also wept again, and said, Who
   shall give us flesh to eat?

5 We remember the fish which we did eat in Egypt freely; the
   cucumbers, and the melons, and the leeks, and the onions,
   and the garlick:

6 But now our soul is dried away; there is nothing at all,
   beside this manna, before our eyes.

To comprehend fully the inner meaning of these few verses, it
is imperative that the entire fable is recognised not as a real event,
but as a major allegory of the mental work, the *Israelites* being a
collective personification of neophytes undergoing the process,
with Moses as the initiate leader. That is why they are made to
wander in the wilderness for *forty* years before finding the *Promised
Land* (accomplishing the process). The 'flesh' in the above verses,
after which the Israelites are lusting, is not real meat, but merely a
word used to express outward thinking. In the course of the long,
slow process, the neophyte must learn to change from outward
thinking (*flesh*) alone to inward thinking (*manna*), at which the
required development of the understanding will slowly be
achieved. But many times, the neophyte will be tempted to
return to his previous, and seemingly natural way of outward
thought (he will 'lust' after 'flesh').

Extending this analogy a little further while we are touching on it, perhaps it can now be appreciated that the 'fasting' so often advocated in biblical texts contains the same hidden meaning, the turning away from outward thinking alone. This is why some biblical characters were made to *fast* for *forty* days (the length of the process).

Thus, in verse 6, the manna appears before the eyes of the Israelites; not their physical eyes, but those referred to by Paul in his letter to the Ephesians, chapter 1, verse 18, the 'eyes of the understanding'.

The catch phrase was used subsequently with great frequency, especially by the allegorical scribes of the Middle Ages – those called the Alchemists. Many examples could be given, like the instances in an anonymous German text of 1625, 'The Golden Tract', where it appears not once, but four times. To demonstrate at least part of this sequence, I quote two relevant passages:

> Tell me where there is sulphur out of sulphur, and mercury out of mercury – or where sulphur springs from mercury, and again mercury from sulphur. When there is placed before your eyes the idea of most fervent love, the male and the female embracing . . .

And later on:

> This matter lies before the eyes of all; everybody sees it, touches it, loves it, but knows it not.

The philosopher, Cyrano de Bergerac, gives an account of a terrible duel between the remora and the salamander, which took place before his very eyes. This *combat*, between a creature of the *water* and a creature of *fire* (traditionally speaking), allegorises the struggle of the Hermetic aspirant as he pursues the mental quest.

By way of further elucidation I add that the Hermetic writers often used the word 'watching' to convey the act of meditation, and therefore the hoped-for spiritual transformation will take place before his inner eyes. This view may explain the words of Paracelsus when he indicated that man must

> . . . be able to turn the exterior into the interior, but this is an art which he can only acquire by experience and by the

light of Nature which is shining before the eyes of all, but which is seen by few.

Elsewhere, this famous Rosicrucian reiterated that man ought

. . . to look with his own eyes into the book of Nature and be able to understand it.

Blindness

A close companion of the 'eyes' code phrase, but in much wider use, is the idea of *blindness*, but here we encounter the possibility of more than one interpretation. In one sense, the inner meaning may be that the blind person so described is a personification of the uninitiated, who cannot 'see' (i.e. understand) the power which resides in his own mind. As a second choice, it can mean an initiate who no longer 'sees' (i.e., comprehends) things by way of information supplied by his physical senses, such as the eyes, but who by means of the process, now relies upon his inner sight (the so-called Third Eye, intuition). An expression of the former may be seen in the biblical texts, where Jesus causes the *blind* to *see*, a statement not meant to be read literally, although admittedly based upon age old methods of faith healing. Jesus (the knowledge) causes the necessary revelation of the inner sight (intuitive powers). A further instance, this time taken from a high Hermetic manuscript called the Story of Nicolas Flamel, concerns a description of a *garden* (the inner mind) in which grew a *rose* (the pure consciousness) tree alongside a *hollow oak*. At the foot of the oak there boiled a *fountain* (subconscious) of the most *white water* (concentrated attention at the second stage) which, although passing close to many people who were seeking it, escaped detection because the seekers were all *blind* (did not know about the mental process).

This 'inner sight' is not to be confused with the seeing of visions, the latter being a psychic manifestation and nothing to do with the higher consciousness. As the fifth century mystic, Dionysius Areopagite writes:

Better to have the eyes open in contemplation than to behold all the angels and saints in heaven.

Iamblichus, the Syrian writer of the fourth century, and one well versed in the interpretation of allegorical emblems, discusses the crocodile, saying that the ancient Egyptians considered it an apt symbol of the process because, not only is it an *ugly monster*, but it is the only animal without a tongue and therefore *remains silent*. Further, its eyes are covered with a thin, transparent film, so that it can *see without being observed to do so* (as the initiate enjoys the higher understanding, yet outwardly appears the same).

Drunkenness

Towards the end of the mental process, the aspirant will receive flashes of intuitional 'knowing', a subtle shift in the consciousness, as his mind touches the realms of understanding hitherto denied him. This shift, well-nigh indescribable, has been depicted either as a sudden attack of dizziness, or a state of alcoholic intoxication. The symbolism is extremely old, dating at least from the times of the Old Testament, and I would venture that the best possible example from that source would be Genesis 19; 30–38, where Lot's two daughters gave him so much wine that he became drunk and they had sexual relations with him. Outwardly incestuous, the true meaning of this little cameo is that Lot (personification of an initiate) drank a quantity of wine (had reached, in the course of the process, the subconscious). This 'wine' was administered by the two daughters who here collectively represent the *Woman* symbol of reflection. When the text infers that sexual relations took place, what it really intends to convey is that the two minds, the conscious and the subconscious, were temporarily joined in a generative and productive manner. The progeny, of course, will be the *child*, or the *new man* of total understanding.

A lesser known application of the symbolism is to be found in the biographical rumour that the 16th century initiate, Paracelsus, was a roisterer and a *drunkard*. The German mystic, Boehme, quotes the symbolism of Jacob and his Ladder to show how he meditated his way to higher understanding, adding

> . . . if anyone will climb up after me, let him take heed that he will not be drunken, but he must be girt with the sword

of the spirit. For he must climb through a horrible deep, a giddiness will frequently come into his head. . . .

(Aurora, Jacob Boehme)

The Beard

With the mental work begun and the aspirant well on the path to the centre of the inner mind, there will ensue a gradual change of character, developing according to the individual ability to reach further and further into the higher intelligence. At the end of the process, he emerges as a completely new personality, the old being completely submerged. The allegories have sought to portray this *transformation* by depicting the aspirant wearing a beard (the *old man*). Sometimes, in order to indicate that the mental work is not far from completion, the beard is described as *long*, *flowing*, and *white*. If the beard is *short* and *black*, it portrays the beginning or the middle of the work. But the man who has completed the process is always shown to have no beard at all. For example, in all the existing portraits of the 16th century Rosicrucian, Paracelsus, the subject in every case is *clean shaven*.

Left and Right

The most straightforward emblems expressing the dual nature of Man's mind are those earlier described, *evil* (conscious mind) and *good* (subconscious). Equally simple, but far more likely to be missed are the terms *left* (conscious mind) and *right* (subconscious), often applied in allegorical works as a movement, or even a deformity, of the main character's body. Any such indications should be carefully scrutinised for a significance other than the mere physical. Mention of the left side of the body – shoulder, arm, leg or foot – may be meant to indicate the conscious mind; the right side, its hidden companion.

I feel it hardly necessary to give examples at this juncture as they will appear self evident in the expositions to follow.

The Leopard

The ancient writers were fond of describing the mental work as a slow 'cooking' or 'boiling' process, by virtue of the *gentle heat* of concentrated attention applied meditatively. As a natural spin-off of this analogy there arose further symbolism featuring bubbles or spots, as on the surface of boiling liquids, introduced to indicate that the mental work was being carried out. In ancient Egypt, many of the allegorical texts featured references to the Leopard, or to the animal's skin. But as you can now appreciate, the significance lies not with the animal or the skin, but with the spots thereon. This particular element of Hermetic symbolism was not widely used, but later period writers, who were themselves familiar with ancient Egyptian lore, did not hesitate to bring it back into use.

Fishing

The Alchemists (initiates) of the Middle Ages allegorised the mental process by making use of the Metallurgists' phraseology, and thus arose the legend that they were attempting to make *gold out of base metals*, creating in its wake a following of greedy fools who, in their ignorance, actually tried to emulate the literal word. The result was months and years of wasted time, spent unproductively over laboratory furnaces experimenting with tin, copper and mercury. Nowadays, the allegory is known for what it is. But not quite so well understood is the way in which the Hermetic writers used the idea of *fishing*, an analogy that can be traced right back to Babylonian times. One faintly familiar application would be that in Matthew, chapter 4, where Jesus, walking by the shores of the sea of Galilee, sees Peter and Andrew casting their nets into the water:

> 19   And he saith unto them. Follow me and I will make you fishers of men.

Soon, along with the rest of the disciples, they were *preaching the gospel* (perpetuating the Hermetic knowledge by means of allegory). Thus, when a text describes a certain character to be engaged in fishing, it may be a covert announcement that allegory is present, that the person fishing is a personification of an initiate. Many times, where this analogy occurs, you will notice that the *fishing* is done at *night* (in the mind), under the light of a *full moon* (meditation in progress).

Summary

Having described the mental process as far as necessary for the purposes of this volume, I now remind the reader that the art of allegory consists of manufacturing a fable in which the process is stylised either by employing a long established Hermetic pattern around which the plot is woven, or simply by the introduction of special, recognised code words – traditional, current, or otherwise – into an ordinary text. In order to formulate an allegory, real life situations, persons and places are often used as a foundation, but with the true circumstances deliberately, and sometimes grossly distorted so as to comply with the requirements of the traditional pattern. Most of the special code words or phrases are of a perfectly normal and innocuous nature when they appear in non-allegorical texts, only assuming a significance by virtue of their careful placing and grouping with each other when built into an allegory. Thus, the major problem facing the student is to distinguish between their normal and allegorical use. I can only assure them that, with practice, the distinction does become apparent.

Any assessment of allegorical literature must be accompanied by the realisation that the peoples of the world are divided into two groups; those who understand allegory, and those who don't, and that the former is infinitely smaller than the latter. Of those who are familiar with allegory, another division becomes necessary, namely those who have accomplished the mental work and those who have not. Again, the former is a great deal smaller than the latter, and in truth, those persons who have managed to traverse the whole way of the process are rare indeed. Fortunately, comprehension of the hidden message occurs at a level of understanding somewhat lower than that of full initiateship, thereby providing a much needed impetus to those struggling towards the ultimate goal.

In the detection of allegory, therefore, care by the beginner must be exercised to distinguish between the writer who truly knows the art, and those who – wittingly or unwittingly – employ the same style of phraseology in an attempt to parody the classic texts.

Using the random examples so far given as a springboard, I now move on to demonstrate how historical enigmas can be unravelled, how romantic fiction can be elevated from the mundane, and how the initiates spoke to each other through the centuries. As the 20th century Alchemist, Fulcanelli, expresses it:

> What unsuspected marvels we should find if only we knew how to dissect words; to strip them of their bark and liberate the spirit, the divine light which is within!.

Chapter Four

Although it would be unwise to suggest that the Hermetic Science emanated from any particular area, be it India, Arabia, Chaldea or Egypt, it is perhaps permissible to state that it was the classic Greek philosophers who developed a style and form from which much future allegory would emerge. The works of Homer, Hesiod, Plato, Pythagorus and Plutarch (not forgetting the Roman, Virgil) are familiar and important names in the philosophic academy. By way of their carefully contrived allegories, many a reader is unwittingly acquainted with the Hermetic Science, with possible prospect of illumination occurring to a lucky few as a result. The message is vividly, if furtively, transmitted in such works as Plato's *Atlantis*, or in Hesiod's *Theogeny*. Ovid, another Roman, but following in the footsteps of Homer, projected it in his *Metamorphosis*, and Plutarch, by relaying the myths of the ancient Egyptians, wove it into his account of *Osiris and Isis*.

Theopompus

As an alternative to the 'death and resurrection' allegory so familiar to us in the stories of Zoroaster, the Gospels, and the saga of Apollonius of Tyana, the Greeks developed a theme concerning a *perfect place*, or *country* (the subconscious), far removed from all known civilisation, glowingly described and accompanied by the strong suggestion that all men should seek out this long lost *paradise*, no matter how hard it was to reach. Readers will at once recognise Plato's *Atlantis* and his *Republic*, along with other notable texts in the same vein, like Thomas More's *Utopia* and Francis Bacon's *New Atlantis*. Much less familiar, but nevertheless in the same category, are the works of Theopompus of Chios, a Greek historian of the 4th century B.C. He collected together a number of extraordinary writings, which he published under the title *Thaumasia* (place of miracles). The collection has long since been lost, but a fragment remains in the form of a dialogue between one Seilenos, and Midas, the king of Phrygia. Seilenos is described as being the son of a nymph, inferior to the gods, but superior to mankind because he is endowed with immortality. In other words, Seilenos is a personification of an initiate of the process.

Amongst the many subjects discussed by the two, Seilenos informed the king that Europe, Asia and Libya (meaning at that time the whole of North Africa) are but so many islands completely surrounded by ocean. Beyond the limits of the known world, however, there was a continent of great magnitude in which lived animals of vast bulk and men of double the ordinary stature. These giant men were endowed with a life span twice that of normal. They had erected spacious cities governed by laws and institutions peculiar to themselves, and *the very opposite of ours*. One of the features of this strange land was that there were two of everything, in reverse of each other. For example, one of the strongholds was called Machimos (the place of war), while the other was known as Eusebes (the holy city). The inhabitants of Eusebes passed their days in peace, abounding exceedingly in wealth, enjoying whatever the earth brought forth without ox or plough, without sowing or husbandry. They were never sick and their passage through life was crowned with smiles and delights. They were so just and without contention or strife that the gods mingled with them from time to time. The inhabitants of Machimos, on the other hand, were the most warlike of men, living constantly at arms, troubling the neighbouring nations with unceasing wars and acquiring empire over numerous states. Few of the two million citizens died peacefully, more often than not falling in battle, overwhelmed with stones or beaten to death with clubs, for they were invulnerable to iron. Gold was so plentiful in their country that it was held in less regard than iron amongst ourselves.

In this fragment we see a remarkable resemblance to the mythical *Atlantis* as described by Plato, and commentators have conjectured that both writers based their stories upon an America as yet undiscovered by Columbus. But we can also quite clearly discern a caricature of the subconscious (Eusebes) and the conscious minds (Machimos).

Another race described by Seilenos is even more strange. These were the Meropes, who inhabited a part of this mysterious continent and who possessed large and beautiful cities. But near the limits of their empire was a place called Anoston, which both in name and character strongly resembled 'that untravelled country from whose bourne no traveller returns'. It lay deep in a chasm, and although no sunshine or pure light sparkled there, neither did total darkness prevail. Instead, the whole atmosphere was filled with a murky haze, impregnated with a ruddy glow. Through this dismal region flowed two rivers, one the River of Pleasure, the other the River of Grief. On the river banks grew tall trees like the lofty plantain, the bearers of strange fruit. Those which grew beside the River of Grief produced a fruit which caused those who tasted it to burst into tears in such an overwhelming manner that death eventually came upon them. The fruit of the trees which grew alongside the River of Pleasure, on the other hand, carried Elysium in their taste and whoever ate it at once forgot all his former desires and every object he had previously loved. The hues of youth came to his cheeks and he travelled backwards along the whole track of his life, tasting boyhood delights for a second time until, at the end, he became an infant once more, creeping back into the cradle, and lastly, seeking as all of us do, that 'narrow house where the wicked cease from troubling and the weary are at rest'.

Whereas the first story is open to something of a literal interpretation, in that it might be construed as an over dramatised account of a real continent, I'm sure that all will readily agree to the second being no more than a fable. Yet, even more clearly do we see the expression of Dualism in the description of the two rivers – the one of Grief being the conscious mind and its outward actions, the one of Pleasure hinting at the beneficience of the subconscious mind and its immortality.

Josephus and the Essenes

Recognition of the Hermetic basis of the Greek works, and the accompanying realisation that such places as Eusebus, Machimos, Anoston and even Atlantis were never real, may provide a reason why no one has been successful in locating the lost continent described by Plato, or its fabled capital city, Poseidon.

Parallels can be drawn with circumstances elsewhere, especially Palestine, where the Jewish historian, Josephus, although known to have been present in Jerusalem only a few years removed from the supposed crucifixion of Christ, saw fit to completely ignore the Gospel incident, thereby creating an enigma which later researchers have been hard put to explain. But to Josephus, the mythical Jesus was only a character who featured in just one of a number of similar allegories devoted to the transmission of the knowledge and therefore warranted no more extra importance than the texts of Plato, Theopompus, or any other Hermetic scribe. In fact, Josephus was more dedicated to the manufacture of his own allegories, working them into accounts of real Palestinian history in his *Jewish Wars*.

One such contrived anecdote shows Josephus to have been influenced by a contemporary, the Roman writer, Pliny who, in a section on botany in his *Natural History*, concealed Hermetic meaning in descriptions of the Peaony, Chicory, Halicacabus, Acacia and Mandrake plants. It must have been the latter that caught the fancy of Josephus, for it is strongly echoed in a passage from 'The Jewish Wars', where the hilltop fortress of Macherus is under discussion. In a rather strange digression, Josephus suddenly writes:

> In a *ravine* which encloses the town on the *north*, there is a place called Baaras (the *warm springs* of Baaru), which produces a root of the same name. Flame coloured, and towards evening *emitting a brilliant light*, it *eludes the grasp* of persons who approach with the intention of plucking it, as it shrinks up and can only be made to *stand still* by pouring upon it a *certain secretion* of the human body. Yet even then to touch it is fatal, unless one succeeds in carrying off the root itself, *suspended* from the hand. Another innocuous method of capturing it is as follows; they dig all round it, leaving but a minute portion of the root covered; then they tie a *dog* to it and the animal rushing to follow the person who tied him, easily pulls it up, but instantly *dies* – a vicarious victim, as it were, for him who intended to remove the plant since after this none need fear to handle it.

No doubt this passage has raised many an academic eyebrow,

because to find such an obvious fable in a text purporting to be a bona fide account of Palestinian history is disconcerting. Interpretation in terms of Hermetic allegory, however, will resolve it at once. Pliny's *mandrake* plant was a symbol of the subconscious, and the root described by Josephus is merely the mandrake under another name. Confirmation of this is given the moment the method whereby the 'root' may be plucked is outlined. The *dog* tied to the root symbolises the conscious mind which, as we have seen, must *die* before the mental work can be accomplished (the root can be plucked). Further enlightenment is to be had by considering the words deliberately emphasised, the certain secretion of the body (meditation) which makes the plant stand still (stills and controls the moving thoughts). The warm springs suggest *water* held at a *gentle heat*, whilst the ravine and the direction *north* indicate the uninitiated conscious mind and its cold shadows of ignorance. The plant is also said to be flame-coloured (red – the last stage of the process) and towards evening (towards the end of the work), emitting a brilliant light (the 'light' of understanding). It also eludes the grasp of many (only a few find out how to develop their understanding by this method).

This quaint little digression, one of several pocket-sized allegories to be discovered within the historian's text, has its merit, but a far more complicated excursion into the mystery language occurs when Josephus sets his hand to a description of the sect known as the Essenes. In a lengthy discourse, we are given a glimpse of a community who bind themselves by rules so rigid that they can only be compared to the inmates of an early monastery. A rigorous schedule is outlined, featuring a spartan diet, the swearing of 'tremendous oaths', and the surrender of the individual desires to those of the commune style sect as a whole. I will refrain from a full quotation of the text as it is easily available, and possibly already quite familiar to most, moving on at once to the special lines inserted by Josephus that must claim our immediate attention.

In the first section of his dissertation, the author tells his readers that the Essenes were always dressed in *white*, and that they regarded the *control of passions* as a special virtue. Then he says:

> No *clamour or disturbances ever pollute their dwelling*. They

speak in turn, each making way for his neighbour. *To persons outside, the silence of those within appears like some awful mystery.*

To anyone versed in allegorical lore, it becomes quite clear that Josephus is here secretly referring to the 'silence' of the mind (dwelling), which must be practised before the process can be brought to a successful conclusion. More hints follow as he explains how the Essenes are *masters of their temper* (have control over their emotions) and are veritable ministers of *peace* (more silence of the mind). They display *extraordinary interest in the writings of the ancients*, especially those concerned with the welfare of the soul and the body (i.e., Hermetic philosophy). They also make investigations into the medicinal properties of *roots* (recall the mandrake), and into the properties of *stones*.

The candidate wishing to join the sect is required to undergo a probationary period of *three* years, after which he must then swear never to reveal their secrets to others, even though tortured to death. (A parallel here not only with the Egyptian Mystery rites, but also with modern Masonic ritual). One of the fixed beliefs of the Essenes was that the body was impermanent, but the soul was imperishable and when once released from its bodily prison, was borne aloft rejoicing (basic Hermetic philosophy).

As I have made clear, it was often the practice of those who set down allegorical works to base their texts upon some real event or situation, only altering details necessary to make allegorical sense at the expense of the truth, and the reader may wonder if it was so in this case. I would suggest that this particular text may have been based on a real life community, extant up until the time that Jerusalem was destroyed by the Romans, and one of which our chronicler would have been well aware: the Qumran Sect as described in the Dead Sea Scrolls.

The Sons of Zadok

As author and scholar, John Allegro, has so comprehensively informed us, this sect, existing from about 100 B.C., seems to have conducted their lives in very much the same manner as the Essenes described by Josephus. According to the Scroll writings, they called themselves the Sons of Zadok, living a commune style of life in the desert and led by a person named the Teacher of Righteousness. Since the name Zadok means 'righteous', it can be assumed that the title Teacher of Righteousness was one that was applied to each successive leader. Any opponents to the sect's religious ideals were personified collectively under the title the Wicked Priest. Even at this distance in time, it is not hard to recognise a form of religious fanaticism and we are therefore not surprised to find that these Sons of Zadok were persecuted by all.

I stress that neither the Qumran Sect or the Essenes, as described by Josephus, constitute an Hermetic Order comparable, say, to the early Rosicrucians. From the outline I have already given, relating to the method whereby the mental process is undertaken and achieved, it can be seen that the process itself is a matter of mental discipline alone. It is not necessary to subject oneself to spartan habits in which the body suffers self-imposed discomfort and even pain in order to attain the mental goal. It is the mind that must be conquered, not the body. Josephus knew this well, and so it is with an enigmatic smile on his face that he uses history, that of the Qumran Sect, to carry his allegory, changing the name to *Essenes* because this, too, contains a secret meaning.

In respect of the above statement, Josephus may have given a strong hint elsewhere in *The Jewish Wars*, when he records that Jerusalem of 54 to 60 A.D. was bedevilled by certain religious fanatics who persuaded large numbers of people that God awaited them in the wilderness, the rough desert country outside the city. In particular, he adds, there was an Egyptian 'false prophet', who collected a following of *thirty* thousand or more, leading them by a *circuitous route* through the *desert* to the mount known as the *Mount of Olives*.

Here we have another blatant lapse into allegory, beginning with the figure three in 'thirty'. The 'circuitous route' represents the reversal (complete circle) of attention necessary, the 'desert' the inner mind engaged in the process, and the Mount of Olives its goal. The latter symbol is arrived at because the oil from the fruit of the Olive tree was used to *annoint* certain people, according to the Bible. You will notice, if you consider this carefully, that all those so annointed are personifications of the initiate. Therefore, to 'annoint' really means to 'initiate'.

Josephus, it is clear, was playing another little allegorical trick on his readers. Even so, there is information to be gained, for these circumstances may lend new insight into the origin of the Gospel story.

The Qumran leader, one of the Teachers of Righteousness, was captured by Alexander Jannaeus and put to death by being hung, or nailed, on a stake, not a cross. This occurred in 88 B.C., and although the Sect survived for a further one hundred and fifty eight years, the event remained in their historical records, as the Scrolls confirm. This 'crucifixion' by Jannaeus may well have been the foundation stone of the Gospel myth to come – although the contents of the four Gospel texts show that the writers drew heavily upon legends whose origins are to be found in Persia, India and Egypt, not upon contemporary events in Palestine.

I add here that a short passage, found in some editions of Josephus, and which refers specifically to Jesus as Messiah, has been recognised by all biblical scholars as a spurious interjection by later propagandists of the dogma decided upon at the Council of Nicea, therefore I have not deemed it necessary to waste the reader's time with it.

The *Essenes* have remained an historical mystery simply because historians have not comprehended that the name itself was coined to designate the adepts of the mental process. Yet clues lie within the text of Josephus and also, if one is prepared to look, in the words of Philo, a contemporary of Josephus. The Semitic source most likely lies in the word 'asa', or 'asya', meaning 'healer', or 'physician'. But other sources will be found in Egypt and Arabia. However, I intend to concentrate on showing how the name was employed from the time of Josephus onward.

The Assassins

Our chronicler takes the trouble to explain how, in his day, Jewish philosophy took three forms. First, there were the Pharisees, who were considered the leading sect because they accurately interpreted the laws, attributing everything to Fate and to God:

> They hold that to act rightly or otherwise rests, indeed, for the most part with men, but that in each action Fate co-operates. Every soul, they maintain, is imperishable, but the souls of the good alone pass into another body, while the souls of the wicked suffer eternal punishment.

The second Order, the Sadducees, did not recognise Fate, but maintained that man had the free choice of good or evil and that it rested with each man's will which path he followed;

> As for the persistence of the soul after death, penalties in the underworld and rewards, they will have none of them.

The third Order was the Essenes as previously described.

It is not hard to recognise something of the Pharisees in the present day Christians, or of the Sadducees in those we call Agnostic, but the Essenes, who are not quite as Josephus saw fit to describe them, remain as always, the mysterious Hermetics. You will notice that both Pharisees and Sadducees are to be found in the New Testament, but not the Essenes, and one may ask why on earth, if they did really exist as they have been described, they were omitted from the divine writings of the Gospels?

As for the name of this sect, we must never forget that Hermetic writers like Josephus dealt in word association, and therefore we turn to a passage in *The Jewish Wars* dealing with another strange body of men called the Sicarii. These people, Josephus states, were *assassins* who committed murder in broad daylight in the *heart of the city*. They would mingle with the crowds at festivals, carrying short daggers under their clothing with which they stabbed their enemies. Then, when their victims fell, the murderers joined in with cries of indignation and through this plausible behaviour were *never discovered*. Apart from the words I have emphasised, finding the Hermetic content in this passage depends upon knowing that the name 'sicarii' is derived from 'sica', a curved knife very similar to a sickle, both of which resemble the shape of the crescent *moon*. Thus, like the mythical sickle of the Druids, the 'sica' is an emblem of the Moon (reflection) and the Sicarii themselves are the assassins (Essenes) who 'kill' (the conscious mind) in the heart of the city (the centre of the mind). As true Hermetic adepts, not as murderers, they existed secretly and so were never discovered.

The presence of a curved knife as a symbol of the moon seems to indicate that the myth had its origins in ancient Persia, the land of the Arabian Nights. Perhaps we shall never know the exact source upon which Josephus drew, but strangely enough, Persia is the scene of an identical legend, set this time in the 11th century A.D.

A feature of Ismaili writings is the frenzied *wanderer who seeks the truth through trial and sacrifice*. Eventually, *one who is spiritually superior* (the inner self) reveals to him *the true meaning* of Muslim Law and Scriptures. Such a *wanderer* was Hassan-i-Sabbah, the legendary Old Man of the Mountains, founder and first Grand Master of the sect known as the Assassins. In his memoirs, Hassan says that he searched enthusiastically for the secrets of science and religion, eventually to be entirely purged and spiritually *reborn*, after which he began to preach the Ismaili gospel. He retired to the hilltop fortress of Alamut, from which base he directed his followers, the Assassins. According to some sources, the Assassins were imbibers of the drug, Hashish (Arabic 'Hashshishin', from which the name 'Assassin' is derived). Young men were trained in combat at the Old Man's fortress, drugged, and then taken to a hidden Garden of Delight, where they lived in ecstatic luxury for a short time, convinced that they had been transported to Paradise. Suddenly, they were drugged again and brought back to the harsh reality of the fortress. The assassination of a designated human target was the price for a return ticket to the Gardens of Delight, a condition readily agreed to.

There is no doubt that, in the latter period of the Assassins' era, this tenet was acted out literally, with planned murder taking place for a suitable reward, but Hassan's sect began with a very different principle in mind. The Gardens of Delight featured in the tradition of the Assassins' recruitment, are to be found mentioned in the Muslim Scripture, the Qur'an, and it is obviously the Arabian counterpart of the Garden of Eden. Scholars have expressed puzzlement that this and other variations of biblical stories should have formed the basis of Arabian Scriptures and, in the belief that the Old Testament stories are an expression of undisputed truth, have assumed that the writer of the Qur'an obtained his ideas from Judaic sources, but misconstrued them. Such is not the case, for the Qur'an is just as allegorical as the Bible, the common factor being that both secretly express the Hermetic theme.

In *The Sacred Mushroom and the Cross*, John Allegro has disclosed the concealed meaning of certain words and phrases within the Qur'an text, although erroneously attributing them to the results of drug-taking. They are in fact Hermetic, referring to the mental work. The *Gardens of Delight*, for example is that perfect place, the subconscious, just as is the *Garden of Eden*, which is why no explorer has found either in a physical location. Another key phrase in the Qur'an is 'wide-eyed houris', supposed to describe the ravishing beauties awaiting the incoming Assassin. In its most basic sense we may interpret this as the *woman* (reflection) with wide eyes (who causes the Third Eye of understanding to be opened), but if this connection is too tenuous for ready acceptance, I refer you to John Allegro's discovery that the phrase has, in its original language, a close word association with an ancient Sumerian root. This same root, evolved into Hebrew/Aramaic, appears in the Bible as the *bramble*, the *thicket* and, most famous of all, as the *burning bush* of Moses. The Language of the Gods is very ancient indeed.

A knowledgable correspondent on this matter has suggested to me that the Old Man adopted the name 'Hassan' because it is phonetically similar to Assassin and also to 'Asasiyin' (those of the *source*, i.e., Essence). Further, that there were two views regarding Hassan-i-Sabbah. One is that he was the organiser of the most successful reign of terror in history, the other that he invented the legend in order to ensure privacy for the school he founded. I leave the reader to form an opinion, but remind all that the myth of such assassination had been written down by Josephus a thousand years before Hassan's time.

Finally, with regard to the use of hashish as described in the Assassin scenario, we must not forget that the word 'khashish' simply means 'dried herb' (dried with a *gentle heat*?), without specification of any particular variety. Certainly the English rendition of today attaches it to one particular form, that of *Cannabis sativa*, but as John Allegro has so rightly observed:

> It is difficult to believe that the 'pot' smokers of today, the weary dotards who wander listlessly round our cities and universities, are the spiritual successors to those drug-crazed

enthusiasts who, regardless of their safety, stormed castles
and stole as assassins into the strongholds of their enemies.

Exactly!. And I may add that a daily intake of drugs does not in
any way develop the *understanding*.

The mystery of the Assassins may be profitably compared with
the motivation behind the bitter struggles which endure today
between rival factions in the Lebanon – a too literal interpretation
of their respective Scriptures.

The Gospels

I anticipate that many readers, except perhaps those whose
interest have kept them abreast of current knowledge and opinion
regarding the Gospels, will have been surprised, if not indignant,
at the apparently cavalier attitude on my part towards the entity
known as Jesus Christ, especially at my insistence on his mythical
status.

I reply at once that the four versions of the Gospel story can be
seen for what they are only after the investigator has undergone a
suitable period of study with the mind completely and utterly
divorced from ideas which centuries of brainwashing by the
Catholic Church have sought to instil. The four initiates who
wrote down the Gospel stories, and whose real names were not
Matthew, Mark, Luke or John, were undisputed masters of
Hermetic allegory, for each version is packed with line after line
of concealed meaning. The inspiration for such a conglomerate of
allegorical scenes did not come solely from the initiates
themselves, for they already had centuries of collected tradition
to draw upon. You have already been directed to the comparison
between the life of Zoroaster and that of Jesus. Scholars have been
surprised to discover that 'virgin births' took place in Egypt, as
well as Persia and Palestine. The 'crucifixion', on the other hand,
has its roots in Indian lore. Thus we gradually become aware that
'Jesus Christ' is not as unique as the Church would have everyone
believe.

What the Gospel writers did was to collect and sift a number of
long-established Hermetic myths and re-write them into a
scenario set in Palestine at a time just prior to the destruction of

Jerusalem by the Romans. Their central figure, Jesus Christ, was so named in a deliberate portrayal of the Dualist idea, *Jesus*, a common first name of the time, being representative of the conscious mind, whilst *Christ*, a word with an Hermetic root, was appropriated to symbolise the subconscious. But the allegorical construction turned out to be far more involved than that, for it is after this basic foundation has been laid that the inspiration of the writers themselves took command. Throughout the narrative of his ministry, Jesus is shown to be a conscious mind that has undergone a certain amount of initiation, for as expressed by the tales of his wisdom and powers, the subconscious is already partially active. The full transmission of conscious, however, does not take place until the advent of a lengthily described 'crucifixion' and *resurrection*, at which Jesus experiences the same immortality offered to Zoroaster. Not content with this, the writers complicated the theme even more by the introduction of twelve disciples, figures who, in their collective sense, portray the conscious mind at the beginning of the process: rough, somewhat ignorant and full of doubts. Thomas, you recall, was not called 'doubting' for nothing. He had the greatest difficulty in believing in the 'resurrected' Jesus Christ, just as the great mass of people today find it hard to believe that they can tap the great powers of their own subconscious. Something of the same is expressed when the querulous Peter attempts to emulate Jesus by walking on water. He sinks, of course, because unlike Jesus who is further along the path of the mental work, he has not acquired sufficient faith.

I may pointedly add here that the word 'faith' is not meant in the sense of blind devotion usually advocated by the gentlemen of the pulpit; instead it refers to a vital and specific state of mind by which the subconscious power can be drawn upon.

It would be possible to dissect the Gospel tracts line by line, interpreting each section of allegory as the story unfolds, but to do so adequately would necessitate lengthy digression into the various historical sources of each segment of myth. Although rewarding in its way, such an endeavour would require a volume on its own and therefore must reluctantly be left to another time. In the expositions of allegories which follow, however, much insight will be gained if certain situations and their accompanying explanations are compared with the Bible, for many subsequent writers of allegory based their inventions upon the myths therein. Remember at all times, that the founders of the Catholic dogma, those who won the day at the Council of Nicea, focused unprecedented attention upon a single, literal interpretation of an Hermetic myth, an action which had the effect of pushing the rest into the far background.

The zealous and often grossly overworked sense of imagination which has endowed the Gospel myth with a sanctification above and beyond all else, must be tamed, allowing a sense of reality to prevail. The myth of the Tiger that Ate Grass has equal importance with the story of Christ in that both secretly express the same *real principle*, showing the way to the real God, not an abstract one.

Keep in mind, too, that the texts which did not rigidly conform to the Catholic conception were either suppressed or destroyed, their authors persecuted wherever possible, and as likely as not, burnt to death in public. Due to this, the words of the Gospels will be more ready to hand than, say, Simon Magus, who stated:

> There is no resurrection of the flesh but that of the spirit only. And that the body of man is not the creation of God; and also concerning the world, that God did not create it, and that God knoweth not the world, and that Jesus Christ was not crucified but it was an appearance, and that he was not born of Mary, nor of the seed of David.
>
> (*Apocryphal New Testament*; page 288 Acts of Paul)

Or the words of the mystic, Dionysius Areopagite:

> Be wary in this work (of contemplation) that thou take no example at the bodily ascension of Christ to strain thine imagination as thou would'st climb over the moon. Heaven is as nigh down as up, and up as down, behind as before, on one side as the other.

Of equal interest, in regard to the allegorical content of the Bible, are some words in *The Sophic Hydrolith*, an anonymous text of the Middle Ages:

> And as the sages say that the above mentioned process of chemical digestion is generally complete within forty days, so the same number seems to have a most peculiar

significance in Scripture, more particularly in connection with the life of our Lord. The Israelites remained forty years in the wilderness; Moses was forty days and forty nights on Mount Sinai; Elijah's flight from Ahab occupied the same length of time. Christ fasted forty days and forty nights in the wilderness; he spent forty months preaching on earth; he lay forty hours in the grave – appeared to his disciples forty days after his Resurrection; Within forty years from Christ's ascension Jerusalem was destroyed by the Romans and made level with the ground.

Finally, there is an enlightening sentence in the Gnostic papyrus *Collectionea Hermetica Volume* (Egyptian Magic), which says:

Ignorance prevails, due to man's failure to distinguish between the true existence, Aionios (GOOD) and the false existence, Hyle (EVIL).

Chapter Five

During his long and diligent investigation into the mystery of the 'treasure' of Rennes le Château (*The Holy Blood and the Holy Grail*), author Henry Lincoln uncovered connections with a little known Rosicrucian Order called the Priory of Sion. Because the basic tenets of the Priory lie steeped in Hermeticism, this lodge is of the greatest interest to us, especially worthy of attention being a list of names, published in the above book, purporting to be a succession of its Grand Masters. Reaching back as far as the 12th century, the list includes a number of historic personages not hitherto suspected of being affiliated to the Rosicrucian movement of the 15th and 16th centuries. Of these, I have selected Leonardo da Vinci, Robert Boyle, and Sir Isaac Newton for special investigation.

Incredibly enough, this illustrious trio are shown in close company with such men as Nicolas Flamel, Robert Fludd and J. Valentin Andraea, men distinguished not for their scientific or artistic contribution, but for their works of Hermetic allegory and especially for their connection to the Rosicrucian movement. That all were involved at such high level with the same covert fraternity strongly indicates that da Vinci, Boyle and Newton were Hermeticists beneath the surface and it only remains for us to examine their writings for any sign of supportive evidence.

Leonardo da Vinci

Information about the boyhood of Leonardo da Vinci is sparse and therefore it is not possible to say with any accuracy if, during his tender years, he was exposed to the influence of an initiate. What can be stated with confidence is that he developed the faculty of intuition to a remarkable degree while still a young man, and that vague traces of Hermetic knowledge can be detected in his famous notes.

After his death in 1519, Leonardo's reputation remained confined at first to the field of art, and by common consent, his genius in this sphere is undisputed. The subject chosen for one of his masterpieces is the Last Supper, a pictorial representation of the scene reported in the Gospels of Matthew and John.

I shall state at once that certain phrases in the texts disclose that the whole scene is analogous to the final hours of meditation before actual accomplishment of the mental process. For example, this 'last supper' took place in an *upper room* (the mind, which is in the head on the upper part of the body). It was in this room that the *disciples* (collectively the conscious mind undergoing slow initiation) gathered to witness the *passover* (transmission of the consciousness to a higher level). Recall that tradition dictates the Passover to be always held of a night of the *full moon* (reflective power at its zenith).

What we wish to ascertain is whether Leonardo was aware that the sequence was an Hermetic myth, and if so, did he reflect this knowledge in his pictorial conception of it.

It is unfortunate for posterity that Leonardo, when embarking on the project, deviated from the well-tried fresco techniques of the time to experiment instead with oil-based pigments. The result was that within a few years of its completion, the original brilliant colours had cracked and faded. Since then, the painting has been subjected to the hands of restorers on a number of occasions, some of whom saw fit to alter certain significant details. In the early 1980s, however, modern art experts began a painstaking restoration of the work, scraping away the dirt and grime of centuries and, most important of all, removing the corruptions perpetrated by the early restorers. Significantly, the plates from which Christ and his disciples are eating are now seen to have highly *reflective* surfaces, mirroring the robes of those nearby, and although only a small detail, it encourages one to look further.

One of Leonardo's favourite devices was the 'pointing finger', a form of mystical trademark by the artist. It appears in his 'Virgin of the Rocks', in 'St. John the Baptist' and is also present in 'The Last Supper', found on the hand of the disciple of Christ's immediate right, from the onlooker's point of view, pointing directly upward. Wherever it appears, the pointing finger is never seen to be directed at anything visible, but always suggestively to a *realm beyond*. The same device was used by Poussin in his 'Shepherds of Arcadia', an artist and work very much involved with the Hermetic story of Rennes le Château. In Poussin's scene, the finger points at a phrase chiselled on the *tomb*, which reads; 'Et in Arcadia Ego' (I too, live in Arcady, i.e., I also have accomplished the process).

One of the most puzzling discoveries made by the modern restorers is that the beard of Simon of Canaan, the disciple seen sitting on Christ's far right, is a deliberate addition. Leonardo, it seems, originally portrayed Simon with only a light chin stubble, not a beard. Not a very significant item, you may think, unless the artist was aware of the traditional symbolism attached to the beard, that it signifies the process not yet achieved. As this is a portrayal of the last hours of meditation before such an achievement, Leonardo might have decided to show his knowledge of the inner meaning by depicting at least one of the disciples as *almost clean shaven*, but not quite. That the other disciples are either bearded or clean-shaven would not alter the significance in the eyes of a discerning viewer of the portrait. Significantly, Simon of Canaan was a *Zealot*.

Unquestionably, Leonardo's most famed work is the 'Mona Lisa'. It may be deemed unlikely that anything of secret significance can be incorporated in the head and shoulders portrait of an unknown woman, but let us examine the evidence.

The first and most striking feature of the Mona Lisa is the enigmatic smile upon the woman's face. It is well known that Leonardo was obsessed by the painting for many years, and perhaps more by the actual smile, for it appeared in all his subsequent work. The onlooker is forced to conclude that it expresses some powerful inner sentiment that the artist did not wish to reveal by other means. It is a *knowing* smile. Sigmund Freud, in his book about the artist, analysed the smile, saying that the figures on which it appeared seem to

> . . . gaze in mysterious triumph as if they knew of a great achievement of happiness about which silence must be kept. . .

Freud then went on erroneously to attribute it to the element of physical sex. Nevertheless, it can be said that his word impression of the smile, from the point of view of a psychologist, is valid and perfectly expressed. Only the interpretation is at fault.

Less obvious Hermetic features are present, the first in the fact that the subject who wears the smile is a *Woman*, one of the classic symbols of reflection. The inference, therefore, is that the enigma, that 'great achievement of happiness', is brought about by meditation. Secondly, it is notable that the distant landscape behind the woman is totally different on either side of her head, with even the horizons being at different levels. The Dualist implication of this is quite clear to read.

Leonardo died in 1519 and in accordance with the terms of his will the collection of notes he compiled throughout his lifetime were sent into the care of Francesco Melzi, a nobleman of Milan. They were guarded with the greatest of care up until the advent of Francesco's own death some fifty years later, at which they became the responsibility of his heir, Orazio Melzi. Seemingly unable to recognise the value of the notes, Orazio allowed inquirers to help themselves as they pleased, with the result that the entire collection was soon dispersed. It was not until 1750 that any effort was made to gather them together again for scientific study.

The peculiarities of the notes have been well publicised – the mirrored form of writing from right to left throughout; the remarkable preconception of ideas later propounded by Galileo and Newton; the prophetic lines, gloomy forecasts of the future which have come all too true. But what we seek is a statement comparable to those of the classic writers of allegory, to show that Leonardo either knew about, or had to some extent achieved the mental process.

Statements there are, but they are exceedingly covert. Certainly the artist appears to have been anti-clerical, for he satirised the Church, its corruptions and abuses. Ostensibly, his quarrel lay only with the material vices of the priesthood, but he made an inner meaning plain by the use of short, carefully placed sentences, such as that which appeared at the conclusion of a passage describing the natural origin of life:

> I speak not against the sacred books, for they are the supreme truth.

It is not hard to imagine the hinted addition; 'if one knows how to read them'. Another possible hint may lie in the sentence:

> Let no one read me who is not a *mathematician* in my beginning.

I have emphasised the word 'mathematician' because, from the days of Pythagorus, two code words employed by the writers of allegory to indicate their process were 'mathematics' and 'geometry', the comparison between these two subjects and the mental work being drawn because they were each studies that took place *in the mind*. Pythagorus, moreover, was an initiate, expounding the Hermetic theme within the framework of his Geometry. Leonardo, as his notes show, continually resorted to sketches involving the theorem of Pythagorus, although to be absolutely precise, there is little in his diagrams to indicate anything more than an elementary level of study.

A more knowing hint is contained within a passage relating to Necromancy, by which da Vinci means the art of revealing future events by calling up spirits of the dead (i.e. as by the Ouija board). Necromancy, he declares, is the sister of alchemy, but is much more worthy of blame because it never gives birth to anything other than lies. Alchemy, on the other hand, works by the simple products of nature, but whose functions cannot be exercised by nature herself because

> . . . there are in her no organic instruments with which she might be able to do the work which man performs with his hands, by the use of which he has *made glass*, etc.

In this whole passage, the art of alchemy is presented as that natural sequence of events which takes place when an idea is born in man's mind and, by manual labour, is then transformed into a material reality, such as the designing and building of a house. However, Leonardo alerts knowledgeable readers to an alternative and secret interpretation by the addition of the phrase referring to the making of glass, a term that will strike an immediate chord with the hardy few who have had the courage to wade through genuine alchemical manuscripts. As an example, Thomas Charnock, the English alchemist of the mid–16th century, was adamant that the services of a *glass-blower* would be necessary in order to complete the process. What he really meant was that the adept must be prepared to make his own

Vase, or *Glass*, both terms meaning the container in which the Hermetic *distillation* takes place, i.e., in the mind. Leonardo, therefore, is indicating that he knew what the real Alchemy was, no matter what impression his words gave on the surface.

The artist seemed to have had no intention of publishing his notes and so a researcher of our particular subject would not really expect to find him writing the style of Hermetic allegory such as we have been discussing, like the Greek myth of *Jason* (aspiring adept) embarking on a *long and dangerous journey* across the *Black Sea* (the mind in the first stage), eventually to bring back the *Golden Fleece* (accomplish the process). The same Greek authors had *Hercules* perform his *Twelve Labours* (collective of the process, just like the twelve disciples) in order to obtain the *Golden Apples*. Apollonius also undertook these *long wanderings*. Can we expect to find a similar work of fable from the pen of Leonardo?.

Surprisingly enough, his papers include a letter, supposedly written whilst he was travelling in Armenia. Called the 'Letter to Devatdar', it describes in detail a visit to the mountainous region there, and especially to *Mount Taurus*. But authorities on the life of the great artist are not convinced that this journey ever took place, despite the seemingly incontestible evidence of the letter itself. Perhaps an entirely new insight on the matter may be gained when I point out that, from a location in Italy, Armenia is in the *east*, and in much the same direction as the *Black Sea*. In Hermetic parlance, the *east* is where the *sun* rises (where understanding dawns), and of course, the colour *black* speaks for itself. Thus it is probable that Leonardo's *journey* was not a real excursion but an exercise in allegory, the more so because the name of the principal destination, Mount Taurus, has two concealed meanings. In the biblical stories, particularly in the Old Testament, you will notice that the prophets have a habit of *climbing a mountain* whenever they wish to *converse with God*. The instances of this theme are so numerous that I have no need to quote any specific example here, but can proceed straightway to the explanation of its inner meaning. It is simple enough: when you climb a mountain, it is a long hard work which demands considerable endurance, but when you do at last reach the top you appear *nearer to heaven* than those below. Thus the fictional scaling of those biblical peaks by the prophets is intentionally analogous to the labour of the mental process. Leonardo's ascent is open to the same interpretation.

The name 'Taurus' is familiar to us as one of the zodiacal signs, the emblem of the *Bull*. In allegorical language, this animal is used to portray the rampant outer ego of Man which has to be overcome and totally subdued before the process can be brought to a successful conclusion. This is why, in ancient myth from Greece and Egypt, you will find the *sacrifice* of many a bull.

The location described in the letter is the great Taurus range of mountains running parallel to the southern coast of present day Turkey. Yet the way in which the artist describes it invokes a curious feeling of déjà vu, and careful research will reveal that the philosopher Plato wrote something uncannily similar when describing the long lost island of Atlantis. Let us quickly compare the relevant passages:

Letter to Devatdar

These peaks are of such a height that they seem to touch the sky, for in the whole world there is no part of the earth that is higher than their summit . . . This mountain at its base is inhabited by a very opulent people; it abounds in most beautiful springs and rivers; it is fertile and teems with everything that is good especially in those parts which have a southern aspect . . .

(*Codis Atlanticus* 145 v b)

Critias

This whole area faced south and was sheltered from the north winds. The mountains which surrounded it were celebrated as being more numerous, higher and more beautiful than any which exist today; and in them were numerous villages and a wealthy population, as well as rivers, lakes and meadows, which provided ample pasture for all kinds of domesticated and wild animals, and a plentiful variety of woodland to supply abundant timber for every kind of manufacture.

(translation, Desmond Lee; Penguin Books)

The main theme of both passages is the description of a place that is unquestionably *good*. Elsewhere than in this book I have shown the Atlantis story to be an allegory of the mental work, and so the possibility that the artist's letter was attempting to make a similar portrayal is strong, providing the almost identical wording is not to be judged as sheer coincidence. Other fragments of Leonardo's letter add to this evidence, flimsy though it may appear on its own, as for example the continuing description of the summit of Mount Taurus:

> And being of exceedingly *white stone* this shines brightly and *performs the same office* for the Armenians of these parts as the *beautiful light of the moon would in the midst of darkness.*

Let me remind readers at once that the most well known of *white stones* is that of Revelation, chapter 2, verse 17, and if you read this verse in conjuction with what we have discussed so far in relation to *manna* and the subjugation of the personality – that which has to be overcome – you will not fail to recognise the connection. The 'beautiful light of the moon', furthermore, can mean the power of reflected *Sun*light (understanding gained from the power of the subconscious by reflection).

A paragraph further on in the letter, Leonardo makes mention of some slight confusion between the Taurus range and the Caucasus Mountains in the north east, for according to many, the Taurus Mountains were also called the Caucasus. To resolve the question, Leonardo interrogated people who inhabited the shores of the Caspian Sea at the base of the Caucasus

> And they informed me that although their mountains bear the same name, these are of a greater height, and they confirm this therefore to be the true mount Caucasus, since 'Caucasus' in the Scythian tongue means *supreme height.*

The reason for this anecdote is to convey a subtle sense of doubt as to where the *supreme height* actually is, saying in effect that it may appear to be in one place, but is actually in another – just as the letter itself appears to be saying one thing, yet says something more to those who are prepared to look beneath the surface.

Certain other passages tend to project similar underlying significances, although, all in all, the letter is admittedly not to be rated as a major allegorical epic. To the discerning, however, it conveys just enough to confirm that the writer is not unaware of allegorical form, and therefore also confirms his status as an initiate.

Finally, I point out that the very name *Leo*nardo (Leo, the *Lion* of the zodiac, the subconscious) infers a connection with the Hermetic Sun.

Robert Boyle

In the case of Robert Boyle, the great chemist of the 17th century, there is much less doubt, for in places his writings exhibit the style and form of classic alchemical tracts. But we may profitably begin by first examining Boyle's attitude towards the Church.

Prior to the age of thirteen, according to his own account, his view of religion was formal and restricted, consisting of a belief in God, who as Providence, watched over the virtuous. But with a move to Geneva, there came about a radical change. One hot and sultry night, he relates, a violent thunderstorm broke, and although such storms were nothing new to him, this one seemed to exert a tremendous influence, leading him to feel that the day of judgement was at hand, and with the realisation that he was by no means ready for it.

> Christ, he later wrote. Who had long lain asleep in my conscience (as he once did in the ship) must now, as then, be waked by the storm.

It is this reference to chapter 4 of Mark's Gospel that leads the informed reader to interpret Boyle's little anecdote not as fact but as Hermetic fable; for if the reader is informed enough to know the Gospels to be mythological, and why, then it follows that Boyle's deliberate reference to it may be indicating that his own words are of the same nature. The relevant verses in Mark are

37 And there arose a great storm of wind, and the waves beat into the ship, so that it was full.
38 And he was in the hinder part of the ship, *asleep on a pillow.* . .

I will draw your attention to the curious way in which verse 38 is worded, the phrase 'on a pillow' being an unnecessary addition to the information that Christ is asleep. Mention of such a *pillow* will inevitably recall the *stone* which Jacob used for a pillow whilst dreaming of his *Ladder,* and shows that the word has a concealed meaning over and above the ordinary sense. I ask the reader to keep this fact in mind, for the symbolism occurs in a later chapter and holds a great significance in a separate incident in history.

Returning to Robert Boyle, it becomes plain that the 'storm' he describes was no meteorological event, but one that took place in his own mind whilst inwardly concentrating (the *hot* and *sultry night,* an inspired piece of analogy referring to the *night* of the inner mind where the two alchemical qualities are to be found, the hot dry and the hot moist). As for the 'storm' as a symbol, more than one recipient of a great revelation has been known to describe himself at the moment of understanding as completely 'thunderstruck', and this is exactly what Robert intends to convey, telling us that his previous conception of God was in total error and that he had suddenly realised why.

From that time onward, Boyle concerned himself deeply with the Scriptural texts, even to the extent of learning Chaldean, Hebrew and Syriac grammar the better to reach a more true translation of the stories therein. Shades of the Mandrake fable by Josephus may be detected in one of Boyle's theological reflections centred about the antics of a dog. When he gave the creature a bone, or a piece of meat, he would hold it higher than it could jump, thus encouraging the animal to try to exceed its normal ability. But knowing that the dog could not reach the food, Boyle would let it fall so that it could be caught halfway. If the dog did not attempt to jump, however, the food was not given to it. In just the same way, Boyle points out, God holds out the possibility of *salvation* (transfer to a higher spiritual level), and the words of the Bible encourage men to reach upwards. God was far beyond their unaided attainment, yet if they truly strove to reach him, he would stoop and give them the prize they could not reach without his help.

Normally read in a moral, or abstract sense, this tale takes on a new meaning when it is realised that the *dog* in the story is the conscious mind, while *God* is the subconscious. The conscious mind can only strive upwards by means of the mental process, and the 'encouraging words' in the Bible are the allegories which tell him to *revere God* (reflect upon the subconscious).

In later life, Boyle was offered holy orders but declined. He did so, he says, for two reasons – one being that he had no other interest with relation to religion, besides those of saving his own soul. The other was

> . . . not having felt within myself an inward motion to it by the Holy Ghost.

This sentence is no more than a succinct way of saying that his own intuition was a more reliable guide to the real God than the meaningless ritual of outward religious functions.

In 1646, when he was just twenty years of age, he became a member of the Royal Society, and makes mention of an 'Invisible College'. It has been wrongly assumed that the latter was the Royal Society itself, the confusion arising because the two bodies were invariably linked by men who held membership in both. To clarify; the Royal Society was a body of the foremost scientific thinkers of the day, a few of whom possessed knowledge of the mental process, while the rest did not. Those who did were known to each other as the 'Invisible College'. In one of his letters, Boyle expresses gratitude that the invisibles now and then honoured him with their company. He describes them as men of so capacious and searching spirits that school philosophy represents the lowest region of their knowledge, and concludes

> . . . with the recital of their chiefest fault, which is very incident to almost all good things; and that is, that there is not enough of them.

In 1645, Boyle had moved to a cottage in Stalbridge, Dorset, where in virtual isolation he pursued not only his material studies, the experiments in gasses that resulted in Boyle's Law, but also a deep study of Alchemy, the mental science. In 1652, he found positive proof, so he later wrote, that mercury could be so purified that when mixed with gold in the palm of the hand, it would generate heat. Two years later, he published a paper in which a story was related by a ficticious entity named Pyrophilus (literally 'beloved fire', or 'philosopher of *fire*', i.e., an Alchemist). Undoubtedly a parallel to Boyle's own alchemical experiments, Pyrophilus described phenomena concerning a *red*dish powder obtained from an *ingenious foreigner* who had visited England on business. Aware that he might not be believed, Pyrophilus had gathered together some reliable witnesses and in their presence, heated a quantity of refined gold in a crucible. When a minute quantity of the red powder was added to it, the gold appeared to change to silver. Pyrophilus pointed out that if gold could be degraded in this manner, then the reverse was possible, just as the Alchemists claimed.

As one can guess, all this is outright allegory pertaining to the mental work, the whole being so cleverly devised that only a complete understanding of the way in which the process evolves will provide the key. To interpret at least some of it we are required to delve again into biblical lore, this time to examine the use of the word 'palm' – for it must be obvious that experiments in Metallurgy are not carried out in the palm of one's hand. The most familiar example of its use is that in the Gospel of John 12, verses 12 to 13, where the crowds hailing Jesus as the King of Israel wave to him with *palm fronds*. This entrance of *Jesus* into *Jerusalem* is, as indicated by Paul (Hebrews 12; 22), not descriptive of a real man entering a real city, but merely another way of expressing accomplishment of the process, the entry into the 'heavenly Jerusalem'. That the palm leaf is so extensively used (the 'much people' of verse 12 of John) indicates it to be a relative symbol of the event – a symbol which is explained thus; in Greek, the word for Palm Tree is 'phoi'nix', a name which is obviously a phonetic companion of that legendary Egyptian bird, the Phoenix, which burns itself to death on its own funeral pyre to rise again completely *reborn* from the ashes. In this manner, the age old theme of *death and resurrection* is related to the ordinary palm tree and is so employed symbolically in the Bible texts. Other facts tend to confirm the association, for the palm tree begins to *produce fruit* only after the first *thirty* years of growth, whilst the tree itself is something of a symbol of longevity, if not immortality, in that it lives for nearly two hundred years.

In Arabic, the Palm derives from the root Q L B, which with vowels added in the appropriate place, yields some interesting results. QuaLB means 'mind', 'heart', or 'contemplation'; QaLaB means 'to reverse', or to 'turn upside down'; and QuLaB means 'to redden' (as in the third stage of the process). It is plain, therefore, that in allegorical parlance, the word 'palm' does not only mean the tree or the flat of one's hand, but also the inner mind.

Boyle's *gold*, which he held in the *palm* of his hand, in other words, refers to the subconscious. The *mercury* that has to be *purified* is analogous to the ever-moving thoughts (like quicksilver) which have to be stilled; the *ingenious foreigner* is the higher understanding, not normally found without recourse to prolonged meditation; and the *experiment* performed by Pyrophilus is the Hermetic process expressed in the allegorical terms of the Alchemist – but in reverse, just to deceive the layman more.

Even more confusing to the outsider is the fact that Boyle waited for twenty years or so before announcing his 'discovery' in a paper sent to the Royal Society. It was to this paper that Isaac Newton gave his now well-quoted reply:

> But yet because the way in which mercury may be so impregnated, has been thought fit to be concealed by others that have known it, and therefore may possibly be an inlet to something more noble not to be communicated without immense damage to the world, if there should be any verity in the Hermetic writers . . .
>
> (Letter to Henry Oldenburg,
> secretary of the Royal Society).

On the subject of contemplation, or meditation, Boyle penned a significant passage, once again drawing attention to a biblical theme:

> A devout, occasional meditation, from how low a theme soever it takes its rise, being like *Jacob's Ladder*, whereof though the foot leaned on *earth* the top reached *heaven*.

Earth is the conscious mind, and *heaven* is the subconscious.

Of all Robert Boyle's writings, surely the section most unacceptable to contemporaries was his 'prescriptions' for the relief of various human ailments. In the true spirit of a mediaeval warlock he prescribed a draught containing powdered warts taken from the hind leg of a horse as a cure for breast cancer. For jaundice, he recommended hanging up the gall bladder of a sheep into which two or three drops of the patient's urine had been introduced. As the bladder dried up, so the jaundice would leave the patient. I quote but three of these remarkable cures, the last being for filmy eyes, requiring that dried human excrement be blown into them two or three times daily. Boyle was not writing with serious intent, however, for these also, are examples of his excursions into the allegorical code. To interpret just one, I select the first mentioned, the cure for breast cancer.

Apart from being the zodiacal sign attached to the *Moon* (reflection), *Cancer*, you will agree, is a disease in which the victim loses his flesh as the cells rot. This unfortunate effect is analogous to the work of the process where the attention, formerly focused solely upon material, outward things, is gradually transferred to the inward, higher intelligence. In this slow transition, it could be said that the initiate 'loses his flesh' (moves away from the physical and material). The breast, as we know, is the organ of the female body which supplies the *new born infant* with milk, a fluid that is *white* – and in classical Alchemy you will find a number of references to something called *Virgin's Milk*, meaning the power of thought concentrated in a single direction during the act of meditation. Boyle prescribed a draught made of powdered *warts* taken from the hind leg of a *horse*, a remedy which is as facetious as it sounds. Warts are blemishes, or *spots*, on the skin, to be compared in a Hermetic sense with those warts on the skin of a *toad*, or to the larger spots on the skin of a *leopard*, while the *horse* is an age old symbol of the conscious mind, extensively used in Egyptian and Indian allegory. Thus the whole rigmarole is a covert reference to the mental work and never meant to be considered in literal terms any more than Boyle's other 'cures' in the same vein.

As a concluding item to this short study of such a prolific allegorist, I revert to Boyle's supposed discovery of a transmutation of silver into gold, as outlined in a conversation with the astronomer Halley, also a member of the Royal Society. Having made this claim, Boyle then went to considerable lengths to have the existing law against the fabricators of gold amended. Under an Act of Henry IV, a person who 'multiplied' gold (by alchemical means) was guilty of a felony, but at the chemist's earnest representations, an amending Act was passed in 1689, repealing the law on consideration that all 'gold' made was to be used for coinage. Certainly, this triumph of lobbying on Boyle's part must have sent him and his fellow 'invisibles' into paroxysms of laughter.

Sir Isaac Newton

This great scientist's fame rests so firmly upon his contribution to our comprehension of celestial mechanics, as propounded in his 'Principia', that equally penetrating studies by him into Religion and Alchemy have been relegated to the background, a regrettable turn of events as far as future investigators are concerned, for the latter subjects are a vital and integral part of Newton's efforts to define the principles of gravitation, and without them his conclusions would never have reached such lofty heights. The way in which they are connected is something to which few material scientists can subscribe, but even Newton – himself beginning from a material viewpoint – was forced away from the accepted mode of thought to be led inexorably to a central principle common to all three areas. It proved to be a fascinating rise through the stages of inner enlightenment.

Biographical data shows that the circumstances of Newton's boyhood subjected him to long periods of isolation from companions of his own age, thus fostering in him the habit of introspective cogitation rather than the extrovert behaviour expected of a young boy. It resulted in an abnormal capacity for concentration being established long before he took his place in Cambridge University at the age of nineteen. His subsequent years there, so it is often related, were marked by the intense manner in which he directed his mind in study, to the exclusion of all else, forgetting even meals and sleep. It is necessary to remark here that one of the fundamental principles of the Hermetic science rules that if the mind is concentrated on a single idea, rather than dispersed among many, then *understanding* will inevitably ensue. Newton proved this to a remarkable degree, for his self-developed ability to focus his attention over long periods – years if need be – gave him access to a higher knowledge, opening his mind to truths far beyond those normally perceived.

By his mid-twenties, he had become fascinated by the enigmatic texts of the early Alchemists, his accounts for 1669 showing, during a visit to London, the purchase of a large collection of Hermetic tracts. Later, he himself was to write more than a million words on the subject, adopting for this purpose in the time-honoured Latin form, the psuedonym *Ieova Sanctus Unus* (God, the Holy One – and also an anagram of Isaacus Neuutonus).

In 1670, to the immense surprise of those around him, Newton suddenly entered into a deep study of Theology, directing all his thoughts towards the problem of the nature of Christ and God. In all likelihood, it was at this period that he began to understand the allegory in the Scriptural texts, but for obvious reasons, the 'heretical' nature of his research would not have been committed to paper open to public view. What he did set down – much of it disclosed only after his death in 1727 – was extremely revealing. His actions at the time, however, held covert significance, for when it became necessary for him to be ordained in order to stay on as a Fellow at Cambridge, he could not bring himself to swear on the Trinity, which he despised. It seemed that he might lose his place at the University until no less a person than King Charles interceded on his behalf, sending a special draft of dispensation to the Attorney General. It soon became official, the terms allowing Newton exemption from taking holy orders unless he chose to do so. He didn't.

The scholar's notes show that he was aware of the way in which the Catholic hierarchy had from its very inception been either unable or unwilling to perceive the allegory that revealed the true religious facts, falsely basing their doctrines instead upon the literal meaning of the New Testament. Newton concluded that the error had begun at the Council of Nicea, a body convened by the emperor Constantine in 325 A.D. to settle the differences of theological opinion between the two Alexandrian priests, Athanasius and Arius.

The arguments of both contestants and the outcome are now a matter of historical record, but Newton had recognised that the entire Catholic doctrine, its tenets and rituals based upon the belief that the Gospels were fact and not myth, had been misleading those whom it sought to teach for more than a thousand years. Even worse, this had resulted in wrongful and bloody persecutions by the Church of the so-called 'heretics', many of whom were publicly burned for expressing the truth.

Of paramount interest is Newton's interpretation of the Seven

Seals in the Book of Revelation. Declaring them to be of a prophetic nature, he maintained that the first Six dealt with religion from the time of its first beginnings up until the establishment of the Christian Church in the reign of Theodosius. The Seventh and last Seal, he reckoned, began its period in the year 381 A.D. and would, until the sounding of the Seventh Trumpet, portray continued Apostacy – by which Newton meant the previously described misrepresentation of biblical text.

> The year 381 is therefore without controversy that in which this strange religion of the west which has reigned ever since it first overspread the world, and so the earth with them that dwell therein began to worship the Beast and his Image, yet is the church of the western Empire and the aforesaid Constantinopolitean Counsel its representative.
>
> (Yahuda MS 1)

Newton's 'Beast' is better known today under the name *antichrist*, but I must at once make it clear that this term has suffered some distortion of meaning by present day commentators. Originally, it stems from the New Testament letters of John, and the manner in which it is therein used is descriptive of the *conscious mind unaware of its subconscious partner*. Some modern writers – so-called prophets – have attempted to portray the antichrist as a living person, or one yet to be born, who will remain hidden from the world, to reveal himself only at the appointed time so that he may wreak great havoc by leading nations into the final Armageddon. This is no more than imaginative nonsense. The antichrist – Newton's Beast – is representative of the fall away from spiritual (inward) thought and into almost permanent (outward) materialism, a direct result of the doctrines founded at Nicea. Subsequently, the Catholic repression of all 'heretical' ideas, both in the spoken word and in literature, effectively brainwashed the masses into acceptance of a Jesus Christ who actually lived and died on the cross, a concept which, due to its abstract pointlessness, had to be projected by force. Thus, all potential understanding of the allegorical meaning was lost, except to the strong-minded few who were covertly resistant to the dogma. As Newton saw it, the slow evolution of man's mind towards his true spiritual goal was temporarily and unnecessarily retarded. Had the Catholic view been correct, and had 'God' been outside instead of inside man's head, there would have been no sign to the contrary. As it is, an intuitive force within continues to make its presence felt, especially materialising in the idea of a Second Coming of Christ, or the Messiah. This concept, projected to this day and rationalised as a reappearance on earth of the long departed Jesus, really indicates that period ahead, after suitable mental evolution has taken place, when enlightenment will dawn, not just to the few, but to everyone – the Second Coming of understanding, when the ignorance of Apostacy has passed.

Newton put as much of this knowledge as he dared into his *Origines*, especially in his references to the meaning of Christ, and what he is made to say in the Gospels:

> . . . Where he speaks of the Gospel of the kingdome, he means the Gospel concerning the future kingdome. . . . So then they are much mistaken who, by the kingdome of heaven in the Gospels, understand any state of men before the Second Coming of Christ.
>
> (Yahuda MS 16)

The Apostasy of the Church, Newton believed, would last until the sounding of the Seventh Trumpet, an event calculated by him to occur in 1867. He was explicit about this – and it may be remarked that the domination of Catholic Rome did begin its decline in the late 1800's.

It was on this platform of higher understanding that the great scientist based his theories regarding the inertial balance that keeps our planets in their orbits, maintaining that gravity was the outward manifestation of an invisible intelligence, not merely a blind, mechanical force. The same proposition can be discovered in his writings on the art of Alchemy. In 1668, when he composed 'De Gravitatione', he also produced two manuscripts on Alchemy, one of which included a brief statement about the inner force:

> The vital agent diffused through everything in earth is one and the same. And it is a mercurial spirit, extremely subtle and supremely volatile, which is dispersed through every place. . . (MS 12 'The Keynes Collection' of Sir Isaac

Newton's works, King's College, Cambridge, by A.N.L. Mundy)

As we have discovered, *mercury* is thought concentrated in an idea, therefore Newton is indicating that the total Universe is the result of an idea projected by a higher intelligence – a concept echoed by alchemical writers of all eras. Further, Newton attempted to explain his enlightenment by drawing a parallel between God and his capacity to move matter, and the human consciousness with its similar ability to will the body into action. Thus, although his dissertation spoke outwardly of a physical magnetism named Gravity, his words implied something more for the discerning reader:

> Here, the question is of a very subtle spirit which penetrates through all, even the hardest bodies and which is concealed in their substances, Through the strength and activity of this spirit, bodies attract each other and adhere together when brought into contact. . . . All senses are excited by this spirit, and through it animals move their limbs. But these things cannot be explained in a few words. . .
>
> (*Fundamental Principles of Natural Philosophy*)

What Newton is trying to say is that the 'vital agent' common to both is the energy of the pure consciousness.

Sir Isaac is not renowned for writing in that classic allegorical form where the process is concealed within a moral, mythological fable, but he did produce essays in the style of the Alchemist, adhering rigidly to the favoured terminology of the Metallurgist and the Chemist – which is, of course, the hardest to decipher. He became acquainted with members of the Royal Society as early as 1669, enrolling himself six years later, after which there was some highly significant correspondence with Robert Boyle, who was at that time Grand Master of the Priory of Sion. When Boyle died in 1691, Newton became his successor in this mysterious lodge of the 'invisibles'.

In a letter to John Locke, the physician and philosopher, Newton penned an interesting post script:

> Mr Boyle communicated his process about the red earth and Mercury to you as well as to me and before his death, procured some of the earth for his friends.

To the Hermeticist, this means that Boyle passed on his very considerable knowledge of the mental work before he died.

By careful insertion of as many broad hints as he dared into his writings, Newton attempted to do the same, but it was a dangerous game at a time when the Church still wielded the power with which to persecute 'heretics', as in the case of the scholar Whiston, a young protégé of the scientist. Whiston held the same ideas regarding misinterpretation of the biblical texts, but rather than keep his opinions within a small circle of friends who would be likely to receive them with an open mind, he put them into print. It was an unfortunate time to do so, for the notorious Doctor Sachaverell, vociferous champion of Orthodoxy, held up the publication as a blatant example of blasphemy and heresy. Whiston was tried by the heads of Cambridge, where he occupied Newton's old chair as Lucasian Professor, was stripped of his post and forced to leave the University.

An example of the caution exercised by Newton under the same circumstances is reflected in his actions when asked by Caroline, Princess of Wales, for a copy of his *Chronology of Ancient Kingdoms*. Alarmed that his original version might be considered too heretical, he hastily produced a shortened paper with the controversial material omitted. Newton was already uneasy with the current public identification of men closely associated with him as heretics because they held the same viewpoint as himself, but it appears that he was too firmly established to be challenged personally.

About the end of the first decade of the 1700s, Newton wrote out his religious ideas in full, returning to an earlier statement that all nations were originally of one religion which he called Moral Law (Law according to Conscience). With statements such as these, Isaac Newton earns the right to be part of this book, although admittedly he was no great exponent of the Language of the Gods. Nevertheless, he dabbled considerably, and perhaps it is fitting to conclude by quoting a further passage about the 'vital agent':

> The general method of operation of this agent is the same in all things; it is excited to action by a gentle heat, but driven away by a great one, and when it is introduced into a mass of substances its first action is to putrefy and confound into

chaos; then it proceeds to generation. . . In a metallic form it is found most abundantly in Magnesia (antimony). And all species of metals derive from this single root. And in this order (Mercury, Lead, Tin, Silver, Copper, Iron, Gold).

> (MS 12 'The Keynes Collection' A.N.L. Mundy)

The 'metals' in the above quotation may require some interpretation; *Mercury* is the attention; *Silver* represents the act of reflection; *Gold*, the pure consciousness, or the finished process. The remainder are explicitly interpreted for us in that anonymous essay of 1625, 'The Golden Tract', which states that, like the three colours, certain metals represent the three stages of the mental work;

> . . . for first it is *black* and looks like Lead, or Antimony; then it is of a *whitish* colour and is called Jupiter (Tin or Magnesia) and this also before it has attained true whiteness, but when it has passed the white stage, it is called Mars or Venus; after that it becomes *perfect*, or *red*.

Chapter Six

Richard the Crookback

Of all the historical controversies bequeathed to us by ancestral England, that concerning the reputation of King Richard the Third has probably been the most bitterly sustained. It is a familiar argument. On one side, the House of Tudor led by Henry the Seventh; on the other, the squabbling Houses of Lancaster and York with their respective red and white heraldic roses. The time is the latter half of the 15th century and the classic argument is this: did Richard kill the Princes in the Tower? Was he truly an evil and malign tyrant, twisted both in body and mind?

The history of Richard's role, first as Lord Protector to the boy king, and then as king himself is too well known to need repetition here. What might arouse new interest, however, is the suggestion that the derisory term 'crookback', employed by certain writers of the period when alluding to Richard the Third, may contain a significance beyond that of mere imputed physical deformity, and that a reappraisal of the epithet may possibly reveal hitherto undisclosed truths. I do not claim, however, to resolve the argument one way or another. Any such enlightenment, if it occurs, will be the sole property of the reader.

Anyone examining both sides of the case for the first time cannot fail to be conscious of the vehemence with which Richard's reputation is destroyed. There is a mounting, vituperative crusade against his name to the point where the modern expression 'overkill' comes involuntarily to mind. Even a cursory examination of documents relating to the period will leave one in no doubt at all that the House of Tudor, once having despatched Richard at Bosworth, embarked upon a sustained programme of propaganda intended to blacken the dead king's name for all time. Lies were manufactured, facts were distorted. Above all, the writers of Henry Tudor's reign were left in no doubt that it would be against their best interests to paint a less evil picture of the departed Richard than their present king would like to read.

The campaign of slander and defamation seems to have been a resounding success, for by the time Shakespeare came to write his version of history into a play in 1597, Richard was presented as the personification of all evil, a monster, 'hunched of back, withered of arm and twisted of countenance'. Elsewhere in the bard's script, he is referred to as a 'poisonous, bunchbacked toad'. Such extremism in the characterisation of a once living king might be attributed to the generous licence allowed a successful playwright. On the other hand, however, there is the possibility that it represents a subtle joke perpetrated at the expense of the House of Tudor, and to find out how this could be, it is necessary to begin at a much earlier period, the France of the 7th or 8th century.

It was at this time that the Province of Anjou, in western France, came into existence, the city of Angers being declared its capital. Our point of interest is an historical anecdote about the son of the first Earl of Anjou, transmitted to us by way of Sir George Buck's book *The History of the Life and Reigne of King Richard the Third*.

One of the first writers to call into serious question the defamation of Richard's character, Sir George wrote his manuscript in 1619, but died three years later before it could be published. His son eventually commissioned its printing in 1646, but not before he took the trouble to delete certain passages. What remains, however, is extremely revealing.

Buck relates the story of a man named Fulke (or Foulke), son of the first Earl of Anjou, who lived about a hundred years before the Norman conquest of England. Fulke, the story goes, was ambitious, covetous, a perjurer and a murderer, but in his old age began to repent. Eventually his past misdeeds played on his mind to such an extent that, to purge himself, he *made a pilgrimage* to confess before the Holy Sepulchre at *Jerusalem*. I have laid stress here because it is only when this point in the story is reached that one can begin to detect the familiar lines of Hermetic allegory. The Earl Fulke, the text continues, performed his pilgrimage under circumstances of the greatest humility, without the normal entourage expected of nobility, passing himself as a common and private person, or as common as one can be with only two servants to accompany him. Arriving near to their destination, it was the duty of one of the servants

> . . . with a cord (such as is used for the *strangling* of Criminals) thrown about his Master's neck, to draw or leade him to the holy sepulchre, whilst the other did acoustre and strip him as a condemned person, and with extremity, *scourge* him until he was prostrate before the sacred Monument . . .

On my reprinted edition of Sir George's work, borrowed from the Public Library, a previous researcher had penned in the margin alongside this tale the words 'a likely story', and while I heartily abhor defacement of books in this manner, I cannot but agree with the sentiment. By now, I hope the reader will have guessed that Fulke never set foot outside France in order to perform his 'repentance'. What he did do was to undertake the mental process. The requisite *humility* of mind, the *scourging* (flagellation, or whipping of the conscious mind's thoughts into submission), the name *Jerusalem* to designate the goal of the higher intellect, all these are well-tried facets of the allegorical theme, an assertion further justified by the way in which the tale concludes. After accomplishing his 'pilgrimage', Fulke is said to have lived

> . . . many years of *prosperity* in his Country, honoured of all men.

Being dragged through the dust of Palestine by a noose round the neck, and at the same time enduring a flogging, is hardly the way, in any right-thinking man's estimation, to ensure future prosperity. It is obvious to me that Fulke found his 'prosperity' in the 'treasure' of his subconscious mind.

The point of this story becomes clear when Buck relates that Fulke undertook his penitent journey using the assumed name of Plantagenet. During the course of his research, Buck came across an early French catalogue of soubriquets, assumed names under which the nobility might shelter whilst engaged in their respective pilgrimages. Among them, *Plantagenet* was listed as the 'plant, or stalk of Broome'. Thus, under the guise of a lowly broom-maker and wearing the sign of the stalk of the genest plant from which brooms were fashioned, and *with which our pilgrim was whipped*, did Fulke undertake his 'journey'.

Attention is also drawn to the fact that the genest plant, in allegorical symbolism, means *humility*, and Buck quotes the poet Virgil (an initiate) to support this, referring to the latter's epithet, *humilis, humilis, genista*. An alternative derivation explored by Buck is that when by the etymologists of his time, who claim the word *genu*, the knee, to be relevant because this is the part of the limb most actively employed in reverence, hence the term genuflect. And this is why the ancient philosophers recommend the genista plant for diseases of the knee. The latter statement is made partly tongue in cheek, for the real significance, as the philosophers well knew, lies in the genista plant as a symbol of *humility*, that subjugated state to be adopted by the conscious mind if the mental work is to be accomplished.

Buck enlists further support by referring to Strabo, who says that the twigs of the genest plant are generally found on a *stony, sandy and barren* soil (the uninitiated conscious mind in the course of the process), whereas other twigs such as the birch, willow and withy, require a watery and moist place to grow. The hidden connection here is that the *scourging* (the *whipping* – the work in progress) with the genest twigs must take place in a region which is naturally *dry and hot*, such as *Jerusalem* (the inner mind 'heated' in concentration). These and other broad hints throughout Buck's text make it quite clear that the author was well versed in allegorical symbolism, and it may give us cause to wonder exactly what was in those passages which his son saw fit to delete. Of more immediate interest, though, is the fact that Buck's statement reveal the House of Plantagenet, descended from Fulke, Earl of Anjou, through the English king Henry the Second, to be in possession of Hermetic knowledge. Whether or not a Plantagenet made use of it is beside the point, although it is worth remembering that somewhere in the Plantagenet line there was Edward, known as the *Black Prince*, so named, as legend has it, because of his suit of *black armour*. What matters is that a Hermetically revised viewpoint can be applied to unravel the absurdities of the Tudor propaganda and to judge Richard anew, for Richard the Third was a descendant in the Plantagenet line and as such, would have been privy to the concealed knowledge. His conduct, therefore, must be reviewed with this in mind.

Perusal of archivic material from Richard's period, that is up until his death, will show that he was most certainly not the black-hearted villain depicted in later works. Quite the reverse, in fact, for he emerges as a fair-minded man, generous, just, and above all, honest. It is admitted that he was anything but gregarious, for he shunned pretentiousness and appeared to others as quiet and withdrawn: a *thoughtful* person. Under his rule, both as Protector and then as King, England was stable and prosperous, an agreeable state of affairs that was later destroyed by the Tudors. In government, Richard sought every possible opinion before making a constitutional decision, rather than acting in a dictatorial manner. This trait that was seen by some as a sign of weakness, since they construed such deliberations as arising from indecision and incompetence on his part.

From the histories of other initiates who lived within the long period during which the Church was a dominant power, we know only too well that such adepts held 'unorthodox' religious views which, in the opinion of the Church, amounted to heresy, and that those adepts were compelled to keep their views to themselves for fear of reprisals. In the case of Richard the Third, very little information is available which may give us some clue to his theological leanings, but it has been said that he was a puritan in temperament. As an example of his no-nonsense attitude to religion, we note that before embarking on the fatal engagement at Bosworth, Richard addressed his troops. At the end of his speech, someone diffidently pointed out that there were no chaplains present to accompany the men into battle. Richard replied that this was as he intended, saying that if their quarrels were God's (i.e., if they entered the fight at the dictates of their own consciences and their intuitional concept of right and wrong), they needed no last supplication; if they were not, such prayers would be idle blasphemy.

It is worthwhile considering that one of Richard's bitterest enemies, and one who later exerted himself the most to drag the dead king's name through the mire, was John Morton, Bishop of Ely and afterwards Archbishop of Canterbury. Most commentators have assumed Morton's deep hatred to have been born of revulsion at the news that Richard had murdered the two princes in the Tower, but existing documents indicate that Morton detested Richard long beforehand, although offering no valid reason. Bearing in mind the long established and active hatred by the Church of any form of Gnostic heresy, and the probability that Richard possessed such knowledge, we may allow ourselves to conjecture that there might at some time have been a private difference of theological opinion between clergyman and king. A careful, but nevertheless forthright man, Richard may have found some way of expressing the Hermetic truth, for which Morton would have every reason to reply with hatred. Such knowledge exposes the literal word of the Bible as without foundation, thereby rendering the religion upon which Morton had built his life as nothing but a monumental error.

Did Richard possess the Hermetic knowledge? In answer, history can attest that he exhibited at least one trait peculiar to those immersed in the mental work: that sense of moral law advocated at a later date by Sir Isaac Newton. At the tender age of eleven Richard was initiated as a *Knight of the Bath*, and while this title has slightly comic overtones in our modern times, it must be noted that the founder movement drew upon Hermetic allegory for its symbolism, for a *knight* is another name for an initiate, and the *bath* is that fountain of understanding hidden within the mind, the pure consciousness. The initiation of the young Richard was, of course, symbolic only, as is the present day rite of the apprentice Freemason. It included the wearing of a *white hood* (to signify a 'purified' head, or mind), a *blue* (same significance as *black*) robe and a token of white silk on the *shoulder*. But we cannot rule out the possibility that real Hermetic knowledge was passed on to Richard at a later date as part of the Plantagenet education. It is worth noting that, in later years, he adopted the emblem of the *white boar*. The boar, or *pig*, is an oft-used symbol of the conscious mind and as the colour white indicates the second stage of the process, Richard may have been covertly claiming some headway in the work.

Historical evidence attests to the fact that he was surrounded by men of learning, as for example John Tiptoft, the Earl of Worcester, a scholar who brought back many valuable manuscripts from his travels. It was brother Edward's court, at which Richard was present, that saw the printing of the first book in England, supervised by William Caxton himself. The choice for publication was *The Dictus and Sayings of the Philosophers*, translated from a French manuscript by Anthony, Earl Rivers.

He had received it during a real pilgrimage to the Spanish centre of Hermetic thought, St James of *Compostella* (compo-stella, i.e., 'celestial earth', the subconscious in the conscious mind).

Sir George Buck, sure that Richard was possessor of the knowledge but unable to say so openly, drops one heavy hint after another in his defence of the maligned king. Discussing one of the slurs cast upon Richard, namely that he was a tyrant, Buck is at great pains to make clear the exact meaning of the word, stating first that in the original Greek sense a tyrant is one who is an absolute ruler, but whose power has not been constitutionally arrived at. In this we see only a reiteration of the main argument against Richard's assumption to the throne over Edward the Fifth, the boy king in the Tower. However, in the 5th Book of his *History*, Buck turns to Hermetic parlance when he states:

> A Tyrant is by another *wise man* compared to a Dragon, who becometh not a Dragon until he hath devoured many Serpents.

He then couples this quotation with the following epigram:

> The Dragon which doth many Serpents eat
> Becomes a Dragon of huge shape and strength
> And so the man that makes his flesh man's meat
> Transformed is unto a Wolf at length.

Historical scholars have, on the whole, been unable to comprehend why Buck digressed into this and similar areas. But a *wise man*, in allegorical terms, is an initiate, and so Buck's use of it sets the tone for the epigram which follows. Buck gives no reference to which it can be traced, but it would appear to have an Oriental flavour about it, in that the usual sign for the Will applied in the act of reflection (a *Woman*, or the *Moon*) has been replaced by a *Dragon*. Thus the epigram tells us that the Dragon (the will) eats many Serpents (conquers thoughts), and the man who eats the Dragon (possesses the will power) is transformed into a Wolf (initiate). This same Dragon, in Buck's reckoning, is equivalent to a Tyrant, ergo, Richard the Tyrant is one who possesses the necessary will power to complete the process. In other words, Buck is saying that Richard was indeed an initiate of the process.

When Richard was slain in the historic battle of 1485, Henry

Tudor ascended the throne of England, and it was then that the propaganda machine was set in motion. By word of mouth at first, lurid stories were circulated, accusing the dead king of assassinating his two nephews, of the callous murder of the mad king Henry the Sixth, and even of poisoning his own brother Edward the Fourth so that he might secure the crown for himself. To complete the picture, there was a suitably horrific description of his physical appearance and demeanour, leaving no one in any doubt that he was ugliness and wickedness personified.

The defamation of Richard's character, in its literary form, seems to have been initiated by John Rous, a Warwickshire antiquary. In his *Historia Regum Angliae*, written about 1490, Rous depicted Richard as a monster and a tyrant, alleging that he had lain sullenly in the womb of his mother for two years, that he was born with teeth and with hair streaming down his back, and that he was 'of small stature, having a short figure, uneven shoulders, the right being higher than the left.'

This attack is as curious as it is malicious, not the least because of the peculiar phrasing. Rous had previously written a glowing testimonial to Richard's benevolence, and while it could be claimed that he did so out of prudence at a time when the king was still alive, the same can apply to the defamatory statements in his *Historia*: he was careful to write something that Henry Tudor would be pleased to read. But what he says must be compared with the works of two other authors, the Bishop of Croyland, who penned a history of the period and who knew Richard well, and Dominic Mancini, a visitor who wrote an account shortly after the king was killed, and who was likely to have seen Richard on several occasions. Neither author made any mention of a deformity, the general consensus of opinion between them being that Richard was quite normal, but a somewhat thin, frail-looking man of little less than average height.

The next and probably the best known contribution to the defamation comes from the pen of Sir Thomas More, but before we examine what he has to say, it is necessary to review an important piece of evidence concerning him.

Thomas More, author and statesman, was only about seven years of age when Richard was killed. Later on, after leaving Oxford, he became a bencher in Lincoln's Inn and then went to Flanders in 1515 to act as an envoy. It was during this sojourn in

Belgium that he conceived and wrote his *Utopia*, a quaint fable telling of 'an unusually orderly state' on a faraway island. As you may by now appreciate, the story is a work of Hermetic allegory and we will now disclose certain key words within its text in substantiation.

The tale of the wonderful and imaginary state of *Utopia* was told to the author by Raphael Hythloday, a man described as being

> . . . past the flower of his age; his *face was tanned*, he had a *long beard* and his cloak was hanging carelessly about him, so that by his looks and habit, I concluded he was a *seaman*.

We have already become acquainted with the 'beard' symbolism, but the other emphasised words have similar meanings so far not discussed. Raphael's face was tanned due to much exposure to the sun, not the physical sun, but the *Sun* of the pure consciousness, and so we are immediately aware that he personifies an initiate in the course of the process. This interpretation is further confirmed by the wearing of a cloak which, in this respect, is the mark of an initiate in the same way as the alchemist's little skull cap, except that the cap is generally of a red colour so as to signify accomplishment of the work, while the cloak is nearly always *black*, depicting the beginning. Remnants of this symbolism can be seen today in the cap and gown donned by the teacher at University and, ironically enough, in the little round cap worn by the Pope.

The key word 'seaman' is more familiar as the figure of the initiate *Jason* who sailed in search of the Golden Fleece, or in that of *Noah* who sought *escape from the Deluge*. Yet more confirmation of Raphael's initiateship is given in the very next sentence, when a friend named *Peter* (otherwise 'petra', the *stone* of the New Testament) states

> But you are much mistaken, for he has not sailed as a seaman, but as a *traveller*, or rather a *philosopher*.

The 'traveller', obviously, is one who undertakes that *journey* in the mind.

After a preliminary discourse about the injustices and mismanagements of our own nations, Raphael begins to describe the state of Utopia. It is an island, he says, its shape being not unlike a *crescent* (the *moon*, reflection), but entry to it is dangerous. The text goes on to describe the hazards – the rocks on one hand and the shallows on the other – and an astute reader cannot fail to be aware of a marked similarity to those phrases and ideas used by Plato to describe Atlantis and Poseidon. By echoing the famous Greek scholar in this way, More is confirming his own level of knowledge and signalling it to others.

Later in the story there comes a detailed description of the people who inhabit the island, a section of land which, readers are informed, was once part of a great continent named *Utopus* (Greek 'outopos', meaning 'no place'). The people all worship in temples designed in such a way that they are a *little dark within*, because it was considered that too much light dissipates the thoughts, while a moderate amount serves to recollect the mind and raise the devotion. There are various forms of religion, but all agree on one point which is worship of the *Divine Essence*. When they attend church, the people dress themselves all in *white*. The priests, however, are robed in *multi-coloured garments* and ornaments which have a *hieroglyphic significance*, representing *dark mysteries*. As soon as the priests appear, the congregation prostrate themselves

> . . . with so much reverence and so deep a *silence* that such as look on cannot but be struck with it, as if it were the effect of the appearance of a deity.

The 'silence' to which More refers is the silence of the quiet mind, the controlled thoughts, called by most Hermeticists 'grace'. Such grace constitutes the pure consciousness, the higher intelligence, which at high points of meditation touch the mind and show the would-be initiate that he is accomplishing his goal. It is the appearance of *God* in the mind.

As comparison has been made with the phraseology of Plato, so there can be perceived a marked similarity with the description by Josephus of the Essenes. They were said to have dressed in *white* and preserved the same reverent *silence* as the Utopians. As before, this deliberate duplication of key symbols reaffirms More's initiate status and it is with this important fact in mind that we now return to his words describing Richard the Third.

More's *History of King Richard the Third* was not published until 1557, but information included with the text indicated that the original draft, when found, had been in More's handwriting, it having been set down, or at least begun, in the year 1515. For reasons known only to himself, More never completed the work and so, commencing with the death of Edward the Fourth, it covers a period of four months subsequently, and then breaks off in mid-narrative at a point just prior to the battle of Bosworth in which Richard was killed. More, being a mere youth when these events occurred, was therefore no eye-witness, as certain passages would suggest by the way they are written. The section now famous for its defamatory nature, and upon which Shakespeare drew so heavily for his characterisation, begins by saying that while Richard was easily the equal of his brothers Edward and George in wit and courage, there was little physical comparison between them, the former being

> . . . little of stature, ill fetured of limmes, croke backed, his left shoulder much higher than his right, hard favoured of visage, and as suche as is in states called warlyke, in other menne otherwise. He was malicious, wrathful, envious, and from afore his birth, ever frowards.

This passage requires careful dissection. To begin with we see that More has followed and even enlarged upon the description given by John Rous. Little of stature Richard certainly was, compared to brother Edward's strapping six feet four, but for the first time in print there is mention of the 'croke back', presumably the abnormal curvature of the spine that warrants the unkind epithet 'hunchback'. It is a matter of public record that as early as 1491 the term 'crouchback' had been attached to Richard, its derogatory use being a feature of litigation between John Burton and John Payntor of York, the latter being accused of uttering it and then adding that Richard was 'buried in a ditch like a dog'. This incident, however, holds no significance for us except as an indicator of the date at which the term was in use.

No one will ever be able to pinpoint the exact origin of these apparent slanders, but it must be held in mind that there existed at the time a certain body of men who were in possession of the Hermetic knowledge, just like the 'invisibles' of Robert Boyle's time. As with present day Freemasonry, they recognised one another by the use of passwords and signs, or by the application of allegory in their writings. I have previously made clear the esoteric meaning attached to the *camel*, and to the animal's hump, and it takes no feat of imagination to comprehend how the latter can be so easily transferred, in allegorical terms, to the back of a human in order to portray him as an initiate. But on its own, this is hardly sufficient evidence, therefore we move on to the next item.

John Rous declared that Richard's right shoulder was higher than his left, a statement which seems to be borne out by the National Gallery portrait of the king. Whether this was a slip of perspective by the artist, or not, must be left to the judgement of the reader, but it is curious to note that in his own description, More *reverses* this sequence, making the left higher than the right. Was this mere carelessness, recalling that an allegorical *right* indicates the subconscious?

Although so far mentioned only fleetingly, the use of the directions left and right as symbolic of the conscious mind and the subconscious respectively dates from an extremely early period, its application being well established long before More's era, and used prolifically since. A claim that such symbolism is being applied in this instance may appear to be made on the flimsiest of grounds, but now I bring to your attention a statement made by the Dutch humanist, Desiderius Erasmus, a pioneer of biblical criticism and a great friend of Thomas More. Erasmus once wrote that More, like Richard, *walked with one shoulder higher than the other*. To my knowledge, no other writer of that period has confirmed this, and while I concede the possibility of two identical deformities manifesting in the same historical event, I am more inclined to the opinion that the phrase was a current recognition signal between initiates, not a reference to a real physical malformation. You have, for example, already been informed of the symbolic wearing of a white token of silk on the *shoulder* at the initiation ceremony of the Knights of the Bath.

The phrase 'hard favoured of visage', in the connotation of those times, was rendered 'warlike', or 'bellicose, one that is always ready to fight, or engage in *combat*'. Other biographies have testified that combat, although not shirked by Richard, was the last thing he wished to enter into and only did so when forced. But the Plantagenets were privy to the knowledge of that secret *combat* which is part of the mental work, and it may have been this to which More was covertly alluding. Biographer Edward Halle indicates that among the common persons of the period, the phrase 'hard favoured of visage' would otherwise have been stated as 'with a crabbed face'. The *Crab*, I remind all, is the zodiacal sign of *Cancer*, which leads us to the *Moon*, and the act of reflection. However, I quickly admit that there is no confirmation of this deduction in More's text. If it was implied, such a conclusion is left to the perspicacity of the reader.

The last item of significance in the quoted passage is the affirmation that, *even before his birth, Richard was ever froward*. The old fashioned word 'froward' means literally 'turned away', or in a direction 'contrary to normal'. The literal interpretation implies that Richard was perpetually perverse, although it is hard to see how he could be accused of being perverse even before his birth. If applied in light of Hermetic allegory, however, it can immediately be seen as the *reversal* ('turning the other way') required in the act of the meditative process. The same interpretation infers that the 'birth' spoken of is not a physical event, but that Hermetic *birth* of the *new man* at the accomplishment of the process.

This conjecture receives support from the text directly following, where More repeats a gossip which has the Duchess, Richard's mother, enduring such a difficult time at his birth that

> . . . she coulde not be delivered of hym uncutte; and that he came into the worlde with the feete forwarde, as menne be borne outwarde, and (as the fame runneth) also not untothed.

In More's Latin text of the *History*, he has sought to clarify the concept of 'coming into the world feet first' by allusion to Agrippa:

> They say, as a matter of fact, that even at birth he was an Agrippa and came forth feet first.

Ostensibly, this is a reference to Marcus Agrippa, the Roman soldier after whom breech (Agrippan) births have been called. Strongly significant, however, is the fact that in the English version, this passage is followed by the words 'as menne be borne outwarde', which somehow implies a death rather than a birth. To resolve this little mystery, we are called upon to remember that the Roman warrior had an earlier namesake, mentioned in

Acts 12 as Herod, but who in fact is Herod the Great's grandson, Agrippa. It was this king, according to the text of Acts 12, verses 1 and 2, who killed James the brother of John, and who also imprisoned Peter. As I have already indicated, the disciples of the Gospels – and this includes the Acts of the Apostles – were not living entities but collectively a portrayal of the conscious mind. Thus when it is said that Agrippa killed James, it is not a physical death which is depicted, but an allegorical one, even though a real king's name has been utilised to convey it. Thomas More, versed in allegory, would have been well aware of this aspect of symbolism, and used it to transmit his concealed message, that Richard was an initiate.

The statement that Richard was born with teeth holds the same deeply buried meaning, but as Shakespeare gives us the best possible explanation of this enigma, I set it aside until the bard himself enters the discussion.

In a few paragraphs, therefore, having laid his Hermetic groundwork, More afterwards goes on thoroughly to defame Richard according to the Tudor mode of propaganda, safe in the knowledge that future initiates would read and know the truth, whilst the uninformed would remain so. Before returning to this main historical theme, however, More apparently could not resist one further Hermetic jest. After discussing conjectures regarding Richard's supposed aspirations to the throne, More relates how 'credible information' was received by him to the effect that on the night Edward the Fourth died, one Mystlebrook hastened in the early hours to the home of a man named Pottyer. The latter's residence is said to be 'in reddecrosse strete without crepulgate'. At his hasty rapping, Mystlebrook was quickly let in, whereupon he informed Pottyer of Edward's death.

> By my trouthe, manne, quoth Pottyer. Then will my mayster the Duke of Gloucester bee kynge?.

It is hard to imagine, More remarks innocently, what gave the man such an idea unless he had some inkling of it from Richard himself.

The point of interest in this offhand item of propaganda is the location of the servant's house. According to the 19th century historian, J.R. Lumby, a Reddecrosse Street did once exist not far from More's own house in Milk Street, off Cheapside. It ran near Golden Lane, ending at St Giles' Church, Cripplegate. Reddecrosse Street is no longer to be seen, but Whitecross Street is, and it was the usual form to have one not far from the other, for as you have no doubt perceived, these two colours belong to the Hermetic stages. *Red Cross* is no less than the Rosy Cross, the emblem of the early Rosicrucians, and it was an established procedure to feature the three Hermetic colours in the naming of places and streets, some of which still remain, such as *Red*hill, *White*chapel and *Black*friars. Similarly, public house signs remain to remind one of a now forgotten heraldic code: *Red Lion*, *Black Lion*, or *Green Lion*. Thomas More, by the insertion of the sign of the red cross into what was very likely a fictional scene, is yet again drawing attention to the allegorical content of his work.

Another covert link with the process occurs in the description of the Lords' assembly at the Tower on Friday 13th of June. While sitting in council, organising the details of the young king Edward's impending coronation, the Lords are joined by Richard. It is *nine* o'clock, and he excuses himself for being late, saying that he had *been sleeping*. After conversing with the Lords awhile, he suddenly expressed a desire for some strawberries from the Bishop of Ely's garden in Holborn; although somewhat taken aback at the request, the Bishop despatches a servant to fetch them. After making the request, Richard then departed, to return a little over an hour later. At once, the assembly noticed a *great change* in his demeanour, wondering at the anger of his countenance, why he was

> . . . knitting the brows, frowning and froting and knawing on hys lippes.

Richard accused the Queen, his dead brother's wife, of sorcery, and to prove his case, drew back a sleeve to disclose a *withered left arm*. The Council were disconcerted at this, for every man present knew that Richard had been so deformed since birth.

The incident of the strawberries has always baffled scholars because of its very triviality; well it might, for it never took place in reality. And as More was hardly the calibre of writer to condone a fabrication unless it served a definite purpose, we should search for a meaning beyond that of the literal. Our attention is at once drawn to the significant colour of the strawberries, red, the Hermetic third stage, and to those who protest at the tenuousness of such a connection I refer to the Arundal MS, a Latin version of the same *History* by More. At this very point in the story, instead of writing the words *fraga . . . nasci* (very good strawberries), More has committed a seemingly astounding error by substituting *flagra . . . mitescere.* The word *flagra* means 'whips', or 'lashes', a clear allusion to the flagellation connected with the Hermetic work, while *mitescere* means 'to grow ripe', a phrase which easily lends itself to an interpretation of the process nearing completion, just as the colour red does. For the initiate who reads the above quoted passage, More's 'error' was no error at all.

The whole sequence is then supported by the cameo in which Richard discloses a withered *left* arm (the conscious mind 'withered', or nearing subjugation), showing it to be another devious way in which to proclaim Richard an initiate. Especially ironic is the fact that the Bishop of Ely – John Morton, Richard's implacable enemy – is made to supply the 'strawberries'.

Undoubtedly, the point of major interest in Richard's saga is the accusation that he murdered the two young princes. This dastardly act, according to Thomas More's account, took place at *night* in the *Tower*, the *innocents* being smothered with their bedding and their *pillows.* Afterwards the bodies were buried at the foot of some stairs

. . . metely depe in the grounds under a great heap of *stones.*

I have previously drawn special attention to the word 'pillow', innocuous enough though it may on the surface appear, showing it to have some significance when related to Hermetic allegory. The pillow, in the cases of Joseph (Gen, 28; 11) and Jesus (Mark 4; 38) represents the power of the pure consciousness, ordinarily perceived in the non-initiate only as the Conscience, as Boyle indicated. The same code word, with a slightly altered meaning, occurs in I Sam. 19, where Saul seeks to *kill* David (the initiate), the latter being *saved* by a ruse in which a *pillow of goat's hair* is employed. More uses the word in much the same way, his whole scenario intending to show covertly that, far from being murdered, the two young nephews of Richard Plantagenet were made privy to the inner knowledge.

What fate really befell them will remain conjecture, as Richard intended, but historians have remarked that while alive the young prince Edward was much more of a threat to Henry Tudor than to Richard, as his continued existence effectively blocked Henry's route to the English throne. Richard was quite aware of this and it would have been reasonable for him to have conceived a contingency plan, ensuring the safety of his nephews should the forthcoming battle at Bosworth not go his way.

It is notable, in More's narrative, that the man named as the engineer of the 'murders' is Sir James Tyrell. According to Audrey Williamson's comprehensive study of the subject (*The Mystery of the Princes*, A. Sutton, 1978), Tyrell was given the sum of £3,000 by Richard, just prior to Bosworth. This sum has been calculated to be representative of the royal budget for a whole year, an unprecedented sum to hand over in those days, and an unprecedented act on Richard's part to do so. Audrey Williamson then goes on to relate a family tradition connected with the Tyrell line, specifically worded, saying that 'the princes and their mother Elizabeth Woodville lived in the hall by permission of their uncle'. The hall referred to is Gripping Hall, near Stowmarket, Suffolk. The author then couples this tradition with More's text in which he describes the efforts made to persuade the Queen to release the younger Richard from sanctuary so that he may be transferred to the Tower rooms to keep prince Edward company, and where the Duke of Buckingham is made to say

> And wee all (I thinke) contente, that both bee with her, yf she come thence and bide in suche a place where they maie with their honoure bee.

In addition to these vague hints, there is the fact that although, when Henry Tudor gained the throne after Richard's death, he pardoned Sir James Tyrell, this magnanimity was later withdrawn rather abruptly. In 1502 Tyrell was tricked into returning from France to London, where he was seized and placed in the Tower. Tried and condemned to death, supposedly for assisting the king's enemies, in this case the Duke of Suffol'., Richard's heir, it is recorded that he 'confessed' to the murder of the princes. It is barely necessary to point out that if Tyrell had undertaken guardianship of Richard's nephews and Henry Tudor received rumours of it, then the only way in which Tyrell could have preserved the safety of his charges would have been to make such a confession, underlining the existing rumour and allaying Henry's suspicion at the same time.

In the century that followed Richard's death, the motley collection of innuendos, vague hints and rumours was fostered and elaborated upon until eventually presented to the public as a vehicle for high thespian drama by the playwright Shakespeare; and therein lies another enigma.

The unanimous agreement by scholars that the writer of Shakespeare's plays had acquired a knowledge of French, Italian, Spanish, Danish, and last but by no means least, classical Latin and Greek, is strangely at odds with the statement of fellow playwright Ben Jonson, who knew Shakespeare intimately, and who declared that he understood 'small Latin and less Greek'. Yet this is no more than a single shot fired in the war of controversy, one side of which alleges that the plays of Shakespeare were really the work of the statesman, Sir Francis Bacon.

The arguments for and against are by now all too familiar and, having no room here to enter into them, I merely point out that Francis Bacon was a noted Rosicrucian, as his *New Atlantis* indisputably reveals. I add that much of Shakespeare's work contains identical Rosicrucian symbolism to that used by Bacon, and thus the possibility exists that Shakespeare was either a Rosicrucian himself, or that he was fed symbolic material by a person, or a group of persons, who wished to remain anonymous. Remarks on this controversy are a feature of *Cosmic Consciousness*, the previously mentioned book written by Richard M. Bucke. It is a worthwhile starting point for those wishing to investigate the subject further.

It is with this as yet unsolved enigma in mind that we now take a brief look at Shakespeare's *Richard the Third*.

The first point of interest occurs in Richard's opening speech where, in reference to his own deformity, he says he is

. . . cheated of feature by dissembling nature . . .

The use of the word 'dissembling' here seems to be at odds with the line of thought inspired by the speech, for it means 'hiding real greatness beneath a deceptive appearance'.

Another quirk of the script is that, throughout, Richard is made to swear 'by St Paul!', and although outwardly hardly of any strong significance to the plot, the inner meaning of such an epithet would be noticed at once by an initiate. Even modern scholars have now admitted that Paul was a Gnostic, and therefore as such would have been an active opponent of Catholicism as it was presented four or five hundred years after his time. Thus the epithet put in Richard's mouth by Shakespeare is a jibe at the Catholic Church.

As everyone knows, throughout the whole of the play Richard is presented as the personification of all *evil*, grotesque and *ugly* in appearance, as malign and malicious as the *Devil*. He is referred to as a *boar*, a *hog*, a *dog*, a bottled *spider*, a *tyrant*, and twice as a 'poisonous, bunchbacked *toad*'. All of these are Hermetic symbols of the conscious mind undergoing the process. He is also called a *hedgehog*, an epithet with a dual Hermetic significance, as it refers to both 'hunchback' and 'hog'. Suggesting that he *hang himself* (undertake the process), the plot happily accuses him of being the guiding hand behind the deaths of Henry IV, Henry's son, Edward, brother George Duke of Clarence, the five noblemen Rivers, Grey, Vaughn, Hastings, Buckingham, and also of the two princes. Thus, Richard is heavily portrayed as an *assassin*.

On the question of Richard's birth, the young Duke of York is made to repeat the rumour that his uncle

> . . . grew so fast that he could gnaw a crust at two hours old.

In Act 4, Scene 4, the explanation of this item of symbolism is given when Queen Margaret, speaking to Richard's mother, says

> From forth the kennel of thy womb hath crept
> a hell-hound that doth hunt us all to death:
> That dog, that had his teeth before his eyes,
> to worry lambs and lap their gentle blood; . . .

By now, the *dog* – and therefore his *kennel* – as a symbol of the conscious mind is familiar, but the *lambs*, an item of biblical lore, refer to the moving thoughts which must be *killed*, or *sacrificed*. Hence the *dog* (the conscious mind in the act of meditation) worries the *lambs* (concentrates on the thoughts) and *laps their blood* (brings them to a halt). As an additional clue, the phrase 'before his eyes' has been carefully worked into the text, supporting the concept of Richard having 'teeth' at birth as being just another way of expressing the fact that he was an initiate.

A clue to this concealed fact had already appeared in Act 4, Scene 1, where Richard's mother bemoans her lot at giving birth to such a son. Talking to herself, she says;

> My accursed womb the bed of death,
> a cockatrice thou has hatched to the world,
> whose unavoided eye is murderous.

A wealth of concealed meaning is contained in these lines, the most obvious being in the word 'cockatrice', a fabulous *monster* like a *serpent*, often confused with the *basilisk*. The latter is famous in mythology because it could only be attacked by using a *mirror* on account of its *death-dealing eyes*. But we must not miss the possibilities offered by 'cockatrice' itself – that is 'a *cock, three* times'. The cock is a symbol of approaching success in the mental work, because it always *heralds the dawn*, and is used as such in the Gospels where Peter is made to deny Christ before the cock crows *three* times, that is before the *resurrection*. The last line of the verse holds an even more powerful indicator, for what is the 'unavoided eye' but a *fixed gaze*? (i.e., the attention turned inwards). No wonder, then, that it is 'murderous' (the fixed gaze of meditation *kills* the conscious mind).

As you will have by now realised, there are many other items of the same symbolism to be extracted, providing the digging is deep enough, but in conclusion, let us glance fleetingly at an anonymous play which appeared in 1594, about the same time as Shakespeare wrote his own version of Richard's history. It is entitled *The True Tragedy of Richard III*, and some believe that Shakespeare based his own work on it. For our purposes, a point of significance occurs when the Duke of Buckingham is arrested and is made to proclaim

> . . . But I am arrested in King Richard's name,, usurping Richard, that insatiable blood succour, that traitor to God and man . . .

the spelling of the word 'succour' here has been faithfully preserved from the original, and as such is something of a curiosity. Spoken, the line would be rendered to the listener as 'blood sucker', inferring *vampirism*, which as you have seen is not without its Hermetic meaning. But if the spelling so carefully retained is not an error, but a deliberate choice, then the sense not conveyed by the spoken word, but *only to the eyes*, is that of Richard portrayed as the *helper of his own kin*. The secret idea thus preserved is that he did help his nephews to escape into obscurity beyond the reach of Henry Tudor.

In Shakespeare's version, this line does not appear, but it is noticeable that when Richard outlines the means by which Tyrell may gain entry to the Tower in order to murder the princes, the information is conveyed *mouth to ear*, in true Masonic (previously Hermetic) tradition.

Chapter Seven

Doctor John Dee

To the casual investigator of historical occult tradition, the name of Doctor John Dee, the Elizabethan astrologer, brings immediately to mind the dubious practice of 'scrying', with Dee himself projected as a rather pathetic dupe of his wily and unscrupulous partner, Edward Kelly, the so-called medium and pretended transmuter of metals.

The generally accepted account left to posterity begins with the appearance of Kelly in the Dee household, presumably as a substitute for the Doctor's first, and sadly departed, assistant in the magical art of crystal gazing. According to Dee's own notes, it all started when his marriage to one of Queen Elizabeth's ladies in waiting encouraged a new found interest in the dreams experienced by his bride and himself. This personal investigation soon led to experiments in the art of crystal gazing, but Dee found that he did not possess the necessary psychic gifts by which such occult phenomena could be induced. In 1581, however, this problem was overcome when a preacher by the name of Barnabas Saul offered to assist the Doctor and act as a medium. Where Dee failed, so it is reported, Saul succeeded, allowing them to hold many seances with the 'great crystalline globe'. Unfortunately, it was not long before Barnabas was brought to trial, accused of other magical practices, and although acquitted, thereafter declined to continue the seances.

The following year a friend brought a Mr Talbot to John Dee's home. It appeared that this twenty-seven year old ex-apothecary, having heard of Saul's departure, had come with the idea of applying for the now vacant position of scryer. Dee accepted and so began a seven year association which destroyed the reputation of a once great scholar.

Talbot soon confessed that his real name was Kelly (or, as some have spelt it, Kelley), and that the alias had been adopted in an effort to start a new life after a disastrous brush with the law. For falsifying deeds and counterfeiting coin, he had been tried and convicted at Lancaster, being sentenced to having both his ears cut off as a punishment and to brand him a criminal. To conceal this disfigurement, it was his habit to wear a black skull cap.

So avid was Dee's interest in the messages received from Kelly's 'angels', and such was his eventual dependence on them, that the Doctor became increasingly dominated by the younger man. Later, Dee reports that Kelly claimed to be able to make gold by using a small quantity of the powder of projection, but that he steadfastly refused to disclose how this transmutation could be accomplished.

The Autumn of 1583 saw the duo on the Continent, and by March 1584, at Cracovia as guests of Lord Albert Alasko, performing prolific experiments in seership, as they had done in England. Eventually, they reached the court of the Emperor Rudolph II, monarch of Hungary and Bohemia, and a personage totally dedicated to the Hermetic art. It was here that Kelly so aroused the king's admiration that the former was made a Knight of Bohemia. Quite obviously their royal host could not have looked more favourably on Kelly and his elderly companion, but relations between philosopher and scryer were becoming increasingly strained, mainly due to Kelly's fits of violent temper on the one hand, and his over-extravagant claims for transmutation on the other.

According to one source, it was while they were in Prague that the attention of the ecclesiastical authorities became focused on Kelly, requiring him to explain away current gossip regarding his 'necromancy'. The inquest was made in the knowledge that neither Dee nor Kelly belonged to the Catholic Church, a fact which made the pair doubly susceptible to a charge of heresy. The story has it that they departed hurriedly from Prague and made their way to Leipzig, thus escaping documented accusations of conjuring. But Pope Sixtus V sent a letter to Rudolph, commanding him to arrest the pair. After much pressure, Dee and Kelly, by now guests of Count Rosenberg of Bohemia, agreed to be interrogated by a prelate of the Catholic Church. During this rather tense interview the prelate wished to know if Kelly's 'angels' could offer a cure for the ills of the Catholic

Church. Dee wisely avoided such a loaded question by replying that the angels had not informed him on such delicate matters, but Kelly threw caution to the winds by saying

> May . . . the doctors, shepherds, and prelates mend their ways; may they teach and live Christ by their word as well as by their conduct. For thus (in my opinion) a great and conspicuous reformation of the Christian religion would be brought about most speedily.
>
> (according to Josten; *An Unknown Chapter*)

The prelate pretended to be grateful for this information, but inwardly he was seething and swore that he would do everything in his power to destroy them.

In 1589 Dee finally broke with Kelly and returned to England. Kelly, however, elected to remain as a guest of Rudolph, seemingly a fatal error on the scryer's part, for pressed by the Emperor to divulge the secret of the Philosophers' Stone, Kelly exhausted the patience of the monarch by his persistent refusal. The hapless scryer soon found himself no longer a guest, but a prisoner, his release assured only on condition that he surrender the information so earnestly sought by the king.

Dee's private diary tells us that Kelly was unable to deliver something which, after all, he didn't possess, and therefore remained a prisoner, an incarceration which lasted until 1597, at which point he was killed in an attempt to escape by rope from a high tower. Falling from a considerable height, he sustained injuries which resulted in his death at the age of forty two.

Dee himself remained in England, first as Chancellor of St Paul's and then as Warden of Manchester College, a position he held for eleven years. Returning to his old home in Mortlake in 1607, he died there the following year, aged 81.

The generally accepted, posthumous picture of John Dee as a gullible old fool, deluded by Kelly and his 'angels', is due to the contents of two books, the first of which is Dee's own *Private Diary*, published by him in 1604, when it is said he suffered much persecution from his Fellows at Manchester College. The second work, put into print fifty years after Dee's death, set the scene for centuries of misinterpretation as to the Doctor's real intent. Edited by Meric Casaubon, and entitled *A True and Faithful*

Relation of What Passed For Many Years Between Dr. John Dee and Some Spirits, it gives excerpts from records kept of the supposed conversations with the 'angels'.

Reading superficially, one would be forced to conclude that the unfortunate Doctor became trapped by his own unhealthy fascination for the art of Kelly's crystal gazing and the mysterious responses from each seance. To be sure, the self-same pitfall exists today, except that the crystal, having gone somewhat out of fashion, has been replaced by the upturned wine glass, by the polished and stencilled Ouija board, or merely with an ordinary pencil applied in the process of automatic writing. Irrespective of the means, the response emanates from the same source, the right hand lobe of the 'medium's' brain, which with the faculty of Imagination no longer subject to the control of logic and reason, fabricates answers at its own dictates. The results have always been intriguing, in some cases astonishing, but seldom truthful. Dee would have been neither the first nor the last to be taken in by it, and thus his reputation was cast into its present unenviable mould. The 'angelic crystal' supposedly used by Kelly – no sphere of polished glass as one might anticipate, but a shapeless lump of rough crystal – rests today in the British Museum, to all intents and purposes a perpetual monument to John Dee's years of supreme folly.

In view of all this, it is strangely paradoxical to discover that modern academics accept Dee's learning to have been profound, pointing out that he was a foremost mathematician of his time, and an eminent astronomer. It is recognised that his preface to the first English translation of Euclid was of considerable erudition, and that the Doctor was responsible for the calculations which reformed the old style calendar. It seems, therefore, that before the above character assassination can be allowed to stand, it would be wise to examine the Dee history in more detail.

In 1542, after some education in Chelmsford and London, Dee went to Cambridge, and here it may be suggested that he set an example later to be followed by Isaac Newton, for during the years 1543 to 1545 Dee studied intensely, sleeping for only four hours a night, resting two hours during the day, and spending the remaining eighteen in deep concentration upon his chosen subjects. The result was an outstanding grasp of mathematics, accompanied surprisingly enough by an advanced mechanical knowledge obtained independently of his studies at the University. Two years later he went to the Low Countries for the purpose of studying navigation and for further investigation into certain branches of mathematics, at this time making the acquaintance of the renowned cartographer, Gerard Mercator. On his return to England Dee shared the fruits of his research, bringing with him the very latest ideas in navigational instruments, the like of which had never before been seen by English sailors. Then, on receipt of his Master of Arts degree, in 1548, he promptly disassociated himself entirely from both Oxford and Cambridge. In a letter penned at a later time, he explained that although both universities were excellent for the teaching of Hebrew, Greek and Latin, the branches of science in which he was interested were not to be found there.

The exact nature of this omission needs no second guess. In 1563 Dee returned from a further visit to the Continent, writing that he had learned more about recondite philosophy there than he ever dared hope, the significance of this statement being made startlingly apparent the following year upon publication of his first major work, the *Monas Hieroglyphicas*. The content of this endeavour was unusual, proposing a formula for a science which seemed to combine Alchemy with mathematics by relating numbers to the Cabalistic tradition, the resulting computations allowing the skilled operator to 'conjure angels'.

Setting aside the introduction of angel conjuring, Dee's work, as a vehicle of allegory, compares with those of Plato and Pythagorus. Dee was a mathematician, but when pursuing that branch of science not to be found in the universities his numbers held a secret significance. Read superficially, however, *Monas Hieroglyphicas* will lead to the conclusion that the author, although learned, was subject to delusive visions. For the benefit of the Hermetically aware, however, Dee took the trouble to preface his book with a special hieroglyph of his own design which he called the 'London Seal of Hermes'. Featured centrally in this frontispiece is the astrological sign for *Mercury*, the Quicksilver of the Sages, encircled by an egg-shaped crest upon which, at the top, sits a *crab* (i.e., *Cancer*, the *Moon*). The whole is flanked by two pillars upon which are mounted representations of the *Sun* and the *Moon*. Comparable symbolism can be found only in the manuscripts of authentic Hermetic authors, and thus by publication of this design, at the age of thirty seven, Dee showed himself to be fully conversant with the Language of the Gods.

In 1577 he eclipsed this work with a comprehensive manuscript intended to cover the whole history and philosophy of navigation. Originally in four parts, the only one now remaining is entitled 'General and Rare Memorial Pertayning to the Perfect Arte of Navigation'. Most assuredly it was a work on the art of physical navigation, but recalling that those mythical heros who personified the initiate were sometimes described in the allegorical language as *sailors*, the use of the phrase 'perfect arte' in the book title is more than suggestive. More commonly it is employed amongst men of Dee's particular learning to designate the mental process. As with the previous volume, the text was prefaced with an illustration of the author's own invention, the Hermetic undertones of which were plain to see provided one had the perspicacity to recognise them.

Some conception of Dee's standing with the leading figures of his day may be gleaned by the revelation that just before Drake set off on his epic voyage round the world, all the influential men backing the project came to see the Doctor. Six months after Drake's return, John Hawkins, a cousin and a close companion of Drake, also paid the 'astrologer' a visit. Dee was an advisor in early attempts to find a north eastern seaway through to Cathay, and it was on his advice that Frobisher sought out a north west passage through to the Orient. Quite obviously these no-nonsense, sea-going explorers didn't seek Dee out merely to find out if the stars were in their favour.

These meetings took place at Dee's home, in what was then the small hamlet of Mortlake, unfortunately so readily accessible to London that the Doctor's studies were continually interrupted by a stream of visitors anxious to view his famous collection of books. He had acquired a library so vast and comprehensive that even the Queen came to inspect it. Especially noteworthy is the fact that, of the philosophical works by classical authors, the largest collection of manuscripts by one writer were those of Raymond Lully, being rivalled in quantity only by those of Roger Bacon. As both these authors were successful Alchemists, the collection of their works reflects Dee's intense interest in the subject.

An interesting example, not just of Dee's expertise with the allegorical code but also of the way in which code words can be transmitted unwittingly by non-initiate writers, occurs in *Purchas, His Pligrims*, published in London, 1625. The author, Samuel Purchas, possessed a copy of a now lost manuscript by Dee in which the Doctor attempted to determine the exact route of Solomon's famed voyages to the mystical Ophir. Discussing this, Purchas writes

> Doctor Dee allowed *fifty* miles a day of requisite way, that is 1,200 miles every four weekes, *resting on the Sabbath*, and *forty* miles a day within the Gulfe, or *Red Sea*; the miles he computeth 9,155¾, and the whole voyage to be performed in *seven* months and six and twenty days outward, and as much homeward; one fortnight of rest after landing before they fell to their *mine-workes*, to be spent in *mind-workes* of devout thankfulness, prayers, festivall, rejoycing; as much before their shipping for return, the rest in their workes and purveying of commodities.

The phrases and code words I have emphasised in this passage are all familiar tools employed to denote either the length of the process, or its various stages, and perhaps only the final example will require an explanation. Among a myriad of other names, the alchemical writers have described the inner consciousness as a *Mine*, because it is where the 'metals' are found. These 'metals' are in reality the emotions, which must be 'smelted' – that is, subjugated and brought under strict control. When this is accomplished, it is said that the whole *molten mass* takes on the aspect of *gold*. It is to this area of allegory that Dee refers in his pairing of 'mine-workes' with 'mind-workes'.

More importantly, I add that *Solomon* (personification of the initiate who *built his temple*) did not in reality go to Ophir in the manner generally supposed. *Ophir*, with its fabulous *gold mines*, was reputed to be in *Africa* (a *hot, dry country*), an obvious line of allegory, and therefore the name is not meant to represent a real place, but that *perfect* location in the mind, the pure consciousness. Of course, the ancient Middle East traded with the African coastal towns in reality, but the journey there was coincidentally descriptive of the mental work, and Dee well knew it. This will undoutedly explain the incongruity of the round trip's precise measurement, even down to the last three quarters of a mile.

The case for John Dee's involvement with Hermeticism is strengthened considerably by the findings of Francis Yates, in her book, *The Rosicrucian Enlightenment*, a painstaking investigation into the elusive movement. Therein the author reminds us that Elias Ashmole, himself a prominent Hermeticist, commented on Dee's journey through Germany in 1589, saying that it caused something of a sensation. In June of that year noted philosopher and alchemist, Heinrich Khunrath, took the trouble to seek out the Doctor, apparently so impressed by the meeting that the Dee influence became plainly discernible in Khunrath's subsequent writings. All the evidence, Francis Yates maintains, points to Dee exerting a very strong influence in an area that a mere twenty five years later witnessed the great Rosicrucian Furore, a event triggered by the anonymous publication of the now famous Manifestos. In addition, it must be noted that Dee's Bohemian host, the Emporer Rudolph, was himself at the very centre of Hermetic investigation, although all the outside world knew of it was that Rudolph spent much time trying to make gold out of base metals.

While recent studies have served to shed much light on Dee's activities during those years he lived in England, similar revelation as to his time in Bohemia, there supposedly accompanied by his partner Kelly, is not yet within the grasp of orthodox historians. Dee, however, left some peculiar signposts of his own, which although no contribution to historic detail, may alter the perspective in which the good Doctor has hitherto been viewed.

With Dee's acknowledged use of Hermetic allegory in mind, we glance at his introduction to *A True and Faithful Relation . . .* etc, in which he writes

> All my life time I had spent in learning; but for this *forty* Years continually, in sundry manner, and in divers Countries, with *great pain*, care and cost, I had from *degree to degree* sought to come by the best knowledge that man might attain unto in the world; And I found (at length) that neither any man living, nor any Book I could yet meet withal, was able to teach me those truths I desired and longed for: And therefore I concluded *with myself* to make intercession and prayer to the giver of wisdom and all *good*

things, to send me such wisdom, as I might know the natures of his creatures; and also enjoy means to use them to his honour and glory.

All classic Hermetic manuals correspond in their admonition to the would-be adept to 'turn to God'. This is sound advice, for 'God' as we know him is that 'giver of wisdom', the subconscious, and it is to this part of our mind that we must direct our concentrated thought if the understanding is to be developed. Dee is here speaking of exactly the same thing, as the key words plainly show, the 'forty' indisputably indicating that the 'best knowledge' referred to is Hermetic. But any adept worthy of the name knows full well that the hearing of voices and the seeing of visions in the form described in Dee's *Relation* is worthless in respect of the mental work. Thus, the carefully placed code words right at the outset are to inform Hermetically aware readers that the farrago which follows is nothing more than an elaborate allegorical joke.

The text of *True and Faithful Relation* needs little examination to confirm this. The process of scrying with Kelly, therein outlined, is ridiculously complicated, requiring the use of a table elaborately marked with signs and seals. A *red* cover of shot silk adorned with tassels was laid over it, the crystal globe in its frame placed firmly in the *centre*, and Kelly would sit down in a *green* chair, whilst Dee himself sat at a nearby desk, ready to write down the incoming messages. In many places, the text is plagiarised from the Bible and, in addition, features incomprehensible languages which Dee calls the Speech of Adam, or the Language of Enoch. And yet the truth regarding the worthlessness of scrying is actually stated quite clearly when, at one sitting, Kelly suddenly announced the presence of a spirit.

E.K.   Now is one come in very brave; like a preacher; I take him to be an evil one.

DEE.   Benedictus qui venit in Nomine Domini.

E.K.   He saith nothing; not so much as, Amen.

SPIRIT.   Are you so foolish to think that the power of God will descend into so base a place?. . . What greater imperfection than to imagine, much more believe, that the Angels of God will, or may descend into so filthie a place, as this corruptible stone is?.

DEE.   What causeth thee to come here?
SPIRIT. Thy folly.

Even in such a brief passage as this, the clues are many. The 'base place', 'filthie place', and 'corruptible stone' are all code words indicating the uninitiated conscious mind, an interpretation which is supported by Kelly when he calls the 'spirit' an *evil* one. The 'spirit' itself is made to state that the power of God (the subconscious mind) is not present in the proceedings, inferring quite rightly that the phenomena emanate from the imagination of the conscious mind alone. The 'spirit' – no Angel by its own admission – is later called by Dee a 'tempter'. It thereafter calls upon Dee to *burn his books*, an easily recognisable code phrase much employed by the adept writers of the Middle Ages and with the meaning that once the mental work is achieved it is no longer necessary to draw knowledge from books (an outward means of gaining knowledge) because the subconscious will supply it (all due to the *fire* of the philosophers).

In common with other initiates, Dee's consuming interest was the establishment of a universal religion, an Hermetic ambition which is made to shine through certain of the conversations with Kelly's 'angels'. In a discussion about the Church, one says

> Whosoever wishes to be wise may look neither to the right nor to the left; neither towards this man who is called a catholic, nor towards that one who is called a heretic (for thus you are called); but he may look up to the God of heaven and earth and to his son Jesus Christ, who has given the Spirit of His abundance and multifarious grace to those who live a natural life in purity and a life of grace in their works.

If you relate the words 'purity' and 'grace' to earlier remarks in this work, the meaning of the passage becomes clear, as clear as the statement that there is in reality one religion only, it being the same for the catholic as for the heretic, a truth only recognised when one has become *wise* (attained a developed *understanding*).

At this juncture I answer the question that must be in the minds of all; if Dee was himself Hermetically *wise*, why did he indulge in such nonsense with Edward Kelly?.

The answer is that he didn't. Edward Kelly, as a real person, never existed, for he was nothing but an elaborate invention by Dee. And to show this to be the truth of the matter, I will now retrace the Kelly story, bringing some pertinent facts to the attention.

After the above statement, it will come as no great surprise to find that the origins of Kelly are shrouded in mystery, and it may be stated with confidence that such information regarding him which found its way into print subsequent to the actual events owes much more to the imagination than to substantiated fact. Nineteenth century writers have attempted to link Kelly with a man named Talbot, who is mentioned in a March 9th, 1582 entry of *The Private Diary*. The initials of Edward Kelly appear on November 22nd of the same year, but there is no sound reason to identify one with the other. It is far more profitable to pay close attention to the words of Dee when he says that Kelly's brush with the law resulted in that worthy's *ears being cut off*, and that to hide the disfigurement, he habitually wore a *black skull cap*. Both these phrases are in the general allegorical scheme of symbolism, showing at once that the literal sense was not Dee's real intent. The latter code phrase is by now easily recognisable, whilst the former should be seen as a variation of Boyle's breast cancer theme, where one is said to 'lose one's flesh', in this case the ficticious Kelly's ears. With regard to the misdemeanour for which the penalty was inflicted, it must have been with ironic humour that Dee named them as falsifying deeds (as Dee was himself), and the counterfeiting of coin (the making of gold).

Kelly's demise is no less allegorical, for as you recall, he *fell out of a tower* and was *killed*. The pictorial design of Tarot Card number sixteen shows this incident taking place: not to Kelly alone, but to any man who experiences the revelation that will follow application of the mental practice. The 'tower' is that rock-hard citadel of materialistic outlook in which the consciousness is imprisoned (like Kelly was) until the advent of a sudden revelatory experience, at which the recipient is said to fall out of the tower. That 'Kelly' was *killed* shows him to be no more than a personification of the conscious mind in the course of the work, a symbol no doubt modelled on Dee's own experience of the process. It seems apparent to me that the Doctor conceived his alter ego on the lines of the disciple Peter of the Gospels, an entity who was ever querulous, argumentative and generally *noisy*, for the Diary reports that Kelly, being younger and easily bored, would sometimes burst into a fit of temper and would have to be *calmed down* (by meditation).

If this assertion is objected to on the grounds that contemporary writers other than Dee mentioned the partnership with Kelly, I would point out that brother Hermetics would treat the idea as a rare and ingenious joke, joining in the fun if the opportunity presented itself. This is especially true of the Emperor Rudolph, who was said to have made Kelly a *knight* (depicting initiateship).

Concerning Edward Kelly's supposed knowledge of transmutation, it is according to Dee that the earless convict found himself one day in the vicinity of Glastonbury Abbey where, by sheer chance, he was shown an ancient manuscript which *no one could decipher.* The innkeeper in whose hands it rested was persuaded to part with it for the sum of one guinea, and thus Kelly came into possession of the *Book of St. Dunstan*, once the property of a bishop now dead, and a tome which contained the secret of the Magnum Opus.

The real life fact is that Dee himself was the visitor to Glastonbury in pursuance of his interest as an antiquarian. In 1574, eight years before the appearance of Kelly at Mortlake, Dee undertook a long tour through the mid-west of England and Wales, eventually moving south to arrive at Glastonbury. His reason for visiting this famous spot was not so much to see the Abbey, but to investigate the great earthwork zodiac of which the tiny village of Somerton is the centre. Dee was known to have held a great interest in Arthurian legends, and when it is stated that such mythological creations are contrived from a Hermetic basis, the Doctor's concern is no longer a cause for wonderment. The secret of the Magnum Opus, the Great Work, is contained in the twelve signs of the zodiac, if one has the key with which to decipher them, hence the so-called *Book of St. Dunstan*, named after the first Abbot of Glastonbury. Of this saint, an anonymous compiler of manuscripts in the 17th century writes

> . . . (he) had no other Elixir or Philosophers' Stone than the gold and silver which by the benefit of *fishing* was obtained, whereby the kingdom's plate and bullion was procured. For the advancement of the fishing trade he did advise that *three* fish days be kept in every week, which caused also more

abstinence, and hence the proverb that St Dunstan took the *Devil* by the nose with his *pincers*.

Outwardly, this passage would hardly connect St Dunstan with the Hermetic process, but I have emphasised the necessary code words to show that such a connection can be made, and in doing so exposed an underlying meaning of the idea of a 'fish day'. I add that the 'pincers' used by St Dunstan would have been the claws of a *crab* (*Cancer*, the *Moon*, reflection).

Thus, the Hermetic tracts attributed to Kelly, *Sir Edward Kelle's Work*, *The Stone of the Philosophers*, *The Theatre of Terrestrial Astronomy*, and *The Humid Path* were in fact penned by Dee himself.

The last remaining point requiring clarification is the reason why John Dee would waste so much precious time on what appears to be an over-laboured, private joke. And again the answer is one of the utmost simplicity, but to find it we need to return to Dee's early years, those just after his first visit to the Continent.

In 1555 Dee was invited to calculate the nativity of Mary Tudor and her husband Philip II, a work which today would be called the compilation of an astrological horoscope. He performed this service and soon afterwards did the same for Princess Elizabeth. But the ever-watchful Church authorities saw to it that he was arrested and imprisoned on charges of endeavouring to 'enchant' the Queen-to-be. Dee managed to clear himself, but was subsequently tried on ecclesiastical charges (i.e., heresy) by the Catholic Bishop of London. The Doctor writes that he languished in prison a long time, 'a bedfellow with Barthlet Green, who was burnt'. In fact, Dee was released without penalty after three months, but from that time on he feared for his life, knowing there would be no second chance.

Already on the pathway to the highest Gnostic knowledge, he now conceived a form of insurance, to become operative should he ever again fall foul of the Catholic hierarchy. By careful portrayal of himself in the *Diary* as a God-fearing but gullible old fool, entirely in the hands of an unscrupulous Kelly, Dee sought to escape the full weight of any further ecclesiastical wrath, deflecting their attention instead to the scoundrel Kelly, if only he could be found.

Only later in life, when he felt a little more secure, did the Doctor 'kill off' his ficticious character, so that he could publish the *Private Diary*. The subsequent scorn directed at him by the Fellows of Manchester College was not unexpected, it being a small price to pay for safeguarding his life whilst at the same time allowing him to proclaim his knowledge to brother initiates.

To conclude this chapter, I submit a conjecture regarding the choice of the name 'Kelly' for Dee's imaginary partner, but in order to project it, I am obliged to return once again to that greatest of traditional allegories, Moses, the Israelites and their *forty* years of *wandering in the wilderness*. I have already explained that their mysterious food, *manna*, is no more than a code word indicating the use of meditation, and I now further draw your attention to its Hebrew meaning, which is 'man-hu', literally 'what is it?'. This querulous phrase has been employed by many an initiate to signify a specific and very important aspect of the Hermetic practice, one of which the adepts never speak openly. You will find the phrase in a certain chapter of the Egyptian Book of the Dead, there repeated over and over again, an insistent message indeed. It can be found in variations of its form in the Rosicrucian Manifestos, and especially in the First letter of Paul to the Corinthians, chapter 6, and I stress that its application is no mere figment of my imagination. The term 'what is it?', or its equivalent, has a very special meaning for the initiate.

Returning now to 'Kelly', we note that alternative spellings of the name have appeared between Dee's time and the present day, but especially the fact that in Dee's original writings, the name is often rendered 'Kelle'. The Hermetic allegoriser's love of word association must be kept firmly in mind as we now look at the common French word for 'what?'. It is 'quel' (pronounced 'kel'), or in Old French of the Dee era, 'quelle'.

Chapter Eight

The Comte de St Germain

If an incorrect and ill-founded assessment of Doctor John Dee's character has been bequeathed to posterity, how much more so that of the mysterious Comte de St Germain?. Where Dee was, at the very worst, dubbed a gullible dabbler in the occult, the St Germain legend has evoked far stronger epithets with that of 'charlatan' or 'swindler' being the mildest of a long catalogue. The principal cause of such vituperation against the Comte is two-fold, due sometimes to the bizarre but oft-repeated claim for his impossibly long lifespan, and at others because of his accredited power to manufacture diamonds, neither of which attributes found any favour with straight-faced historians bent on compiling an acceptably factual dossier of his life and times. The fact that St Germain was wealthy and well bred, that he travelled extensively, had almost magical access to high places, and somehow contrived to be on the spot at the advent of certain historical occasions, raises no objection from the scribes. But guaranteed to being an immediate scowl of frustration to their scholarly brows, are the persistent and unaccountable legends that the Comte had found not only the Elixir of Life, but the Philosophers' Stone as well. Worse still was the added fact that the memoirs of a number of indisputably reputable persons appeared to uphold such fanciful fairy tales.

Having the advantage of now knowing exactly what this mysterious Stone of the Philosophers really is, we can at once recognise that the historical scribes were encountering the ever-present stumbling block of Hermetic allegory – and were failing to circumvent it. Not hampered by the same handicap, it is possible here to detect and interpret the Hermetic material, thereby placing the shadowy figure of St Germain in its proper perspective.

At least half the available historic data regarding the Comte has been brought to light by the extensive research carried out at the beginning of this century by Isabel Cooper-Oakley, who travelled widely to peruse personal diaries, archivic material and even diplomatic correspondence, a painstaking work which culminated in the publication of *The Count of St. Germain*, in Milan, 1912. This interesting document, reprinted in 1970 and therefore still available to modern readers, offers a comprehensive portrait of St Germain from various points of view, as is indicated by an impressive bibliography. However, it is necessary at the outset to make two important notes in respect of these sources.

First, it must always be held in mind that St Germain was a noted and very highly placed Rosicrucian. Just as in any other age, Society in the mid-18th century unknowingly nurtured amongst them an elite few who possessed Hermetic knowledge and who were accordingly most adept in the art of allegory. Certain authors who recorded the Comte's activities were themselves members of either the same Order, or of one closely affiliated, and thus any Hermetic fables fabricated at the time, either by the Comte himself or by his fraternal brothers, may well be incorporated in those writings left to posterity. It is the responsibility of the reader to recognise them for what they are.

Secondly, a certain amount of material reproduced by Isabel Cooper-Oakley has been taken from *Souvenirs sur Marie-Antoinette*, (1836), supposedly the diary of one Countess d'Adhemar, who is represented as one of the ladies in waiting at the court of Versailles. Doubtless accepted in good faith by Isabel Cooper-Oakley, subsequent investigation has revealed this material to be a fabrication, for although there had been a Comte d'Adhemar close to those at Versailles, no woman of that name was attached to the court. G.B. Voltz, author of *Der Graf von Saint-Germain* (1923), maintains that the Countess d'Adhemar was a ficticious person invented by an anonymous novelist. The French writer, Etienne Leon de Lamothe-Langon supports this claim, stating that the *Souvenirs* were a fabrication; thus this part of Isabel Cooper-Oakley's book can be discounted for the purposes of our investigation.

The stories about the Comte's longevity seem to emanate from one particular event and therefore we commence with an examination of the relevant source.

From an 1864 publication of anecdotes written by an un-named and widowed Countess concerning events taking place at the courts of Louis 14th, 15th and 16th, comes the intriguing story of the elderly Countess von Georgy. While at the court of Louis 15th, in 1743, she was introduced to an imposing newcomer to royal circles, the Comte de St Germain, but after the initial exchange of pleasantries was over and the Comte had moved on to talk with others, she continued to eye the Comte with an air of puzzlement and curiosity. Finally, she reapproached him and asked if his father had been in Venice in 1710, as she was certain that she had known him. The Comte replied in the negative, but went on to say that he himself had been living in Venice at the time specified and that he had enjoyed the honour of knowing the Countess then. He added that they used to enjoy musical interludes together, he playing the piano while she sang. The Countess shook her head and declared that such a thing was not possible.

'The St Germain I knew in those days,' she said. 'Was at least forty five years old, and you are hardly more than that now!.'

The Comte smiled and murmured that he was very old, but Madame von Georgy would not consider the idea. St Germain then recounted a number of details connected with their earlier meeting personal to them both, adding that if she still doubted, he could relate even more circumstances and conversations. But the Countess interrupted him:

'No, no!,' she said. 'I am convinced. You are a most extraordinary man . . . a devil!.'

At this last remark the Comte threw up his hands in horror.

'For pity's sake!,' he exclaimed. 'No such names!.' He appeared to be seized with a fit of trembling in his limbs and made a hurried exit.

Isabel Cooper-Oakley indicates that this interlude was not set down at the time, but only after six or seven years had elapsed, thus permitting the factor of a faulty memory to be added to the possibility of a slightly over-worked imagination. My own opinion is that the incident described is an invention – up to a point – for I do not preclude the author being influenced by certain, more informative accounts circulating at the time. As an instance, the memoirs of a fellow member of the royal court, the Baron de Gleichen, yields the following reminiscence:

> I have heard Rameau and an old relative of a French ambassador at Venice testify to having known M. de St. Germain in 1710, when he had the appearance of a man of fifty years of age.

Jean Philippe Rameau, of course, was a prominent classical composer of the period and would have been sixty years of age in 1743. He too, was a favoured visitor to the court and therefore no stranger to the Baron.

Investigators into the St Germain enigma have examined the words of both the above diarists, tending quite naturally to place more reliability on the de Gleichen account, concluding that St Germain must have been in his eighties in 1743. This was perplexing because evidence of an even more reliable nature indicated that the Comte died in 1784, a fact which left them with no alternative but to assume that he reached the ripe old age of 124. And while such advanced years are by no means beyond the bounds of possibility, the known fact that the Comte was still actively travelling from town to town up to five years before his demise, renders the improbability uncomfortably high. The investigators, however, obviously unfamiliar with the allegorical devices of the time, have remained unaware that a single sentence in the words of Baron de Gleichen renders their calculations invalid.

One method of referring to a brother initiate frequently resorted to by Hermetic writers of the 15th and 16th centuries was to use the phrase 'a man of fifty', the *fifty* being one of several well-established ways to express the length of time taken by the process. Therefore, for one adept to say that a person looked like 'a man of fifty' was for him to indicate covertly that the subject was a man of the process – an initiate. And it is in this time-honoured manner that the Baron was reaffirming St Germain's high philosophical status. Whether it was the Baron himself who held the key to allegory and made use of it at the time of writing, or if the coded phrase was actually spoken by Rameau and his unidentified companion, is not possible to say, but either one or all of the trio could have been a knowledgeable member of a Rosicrucian or Freemasons lodge, and therefore a fraternal brother of the Comte. What remains is the fact that the sentence in the Baron's memoirs has nothing to do with St Germain's age.

The Hermetic viewpoint, I further suggest, would tend to throw light on the rather irrational conclusion to the Madame von Georgy episode, where the Comte is recorded as showing visible signs of revulsion at the mere mention of the epithet 'devil'. That this is something that would have occurred in real life is highly unlikely, and so lends disbelief to the whole story. But if this *devil* is thought of in terms of analogous to the conscious mind, whilst the figure of the Comte personifies the pure consciousness, then some sense is immediately imparted to it, for in the course of the mental work, the pure consciousness will recoil at the very first contact. Admittedly the analogy is obscure and only perceptible to those who have worked to develop their understanding of allegorical lore, but the real mystery is how it came to be present in what is no more than a compendium of court gossip. If not deliberately contrived by the writer, it serves once again to illustrate the inadvertant transmission of Hermetic truth, picked up from fragments of initiate-conceived myth and relayed by way of imaginative fiction.

That St Germain was a Rosicrucian, highly esteemed by fellow lodge members, there is no doubt, judging by the testimony of various persons highly placed in Masonic circles, but such attestation is meaningless unless the writers themselves have acquired access to the intricacies of the allegorical code. Only by the competent use of allegory by the authors, can readers of later times be assured that the information conveyed is genuine, and as an example, I turn to a letter culled from the memoirs of the Graf Philippe Cobenzl, quoted by Isabel Cooper-Oakley. Written in Brussels by an earlier namesake of the biographer, Graf Karl Cobenzl, it is addressed to Prince Kaunitz, 'the Prime Minister' and dated April 8th 1763.

Opening with the news that the Comte de St Germain had passed his way some three months previously, the writer proceeds to an enthusiastic description of his famed guest, stating that although possessing great wealth, the Comte's style of living was nevertheless one of the greatest simplicity. Then the writer adds

> . . . he *knows everything*, and shows an uprightness, a *goodness of soul*, worthy of admiration. Among a number of

> his accomplishments, he made *under my own eyes*, some
> experiments, of which the most important were the
> *transmutation of iron into a metal as beautiful as gold.* . .

Karl's permutation of the familiar Hermetic catch phrase
'before your very eyes' at once alerts knowledgeable readers to be
on guard for possible allegory – a possibility which becomes a
reality in the very next sentence with the reference to a
'transmutation' into *gold.* Having thus forewarned readers, the
letter continues, outlining the Comte's further accomplishments
– a masterly ability to dye skins and tan them to perfection, the
same high skill being extended to the dyeing of silks, the
composition of colours for art, and even the removal of odour
from artists' oils. All these marvels, Karl reiterates, were carried
out *under his own eyes*, his account so glowing that one is left in no
doubt that the Comte was a veritable genius, the possible profits
of a commercial enterprise with him being – in the writer's own
words – 'up to millions'.

It is passages such as these, consistently misunderstood by
biographers, that have lent substance to the many accusations of
confidence trickery levelled against St Germain, a continuing slur
on a reputation no doubt made questionable in the first instance
by the Comte's own claim to be able to manufacture diamonds.
We must never forget, therefore, that we are dealing with subtle
allegory.

Karl was thoroughly convinced of his guest's honesty and
trustworthiness:

> . . . I have endeavoured to take advantage of the friendship
> that this man has felt for me, and to learn from him all these
> secrets. He has given them to me, and asks nothing for
> himself beyond a payment proportionate to the profits that
> may accrue from them, it being understood that this shall be
> only when the profit has been made.

Nevertheless, Karl took precautions:

> As the marvellous must inevitably seem uncertain, I have
> avoided the two points which appear to me to be feared, the
> first, the being of a dupe, and the second, the involving
> myself in too great an expenditure.

Both pitfalls were satisfactorily negotiated, the first being resolved on the expert opinion of a trusted friend, *under whose eyes* the requisite procedures were tried, tested and proved to be all that the Comte claimed. Thus, Karl concluded, at minimal expense and even less risk, the moment for deriving profit was already close at hand.

It will not have escaped the reader's attention that our code phrase has been employed *three* times in the course of Karl's letter, an even surer indication that the text is not to be read literally. And indeed, the first application of the phrase is no more than an introduction to a wealth of covert meaning worked into the list of the Comte's so-called accomplishments: the dyeing of woods and silks, the composition of colours, and the expert tanning of skins. As in the field of Metallurgy and Chemistry, with its jargon names of 'calcination', 'distillation', 'sublimation' – each of which have been given hidden significance by the allegorical masters – so the occupations accredited to St Germain have similarly been adapted at one time or another.

I suspect that the 'composition of colours' would be the easiest to relate to the Hermeticist, for the adept has often been termed an 'artist' since he deals in *colours* (i.e., the three Hermetic colours representing the stages of the Work). I would think the passage most familiar to all in which the colours play a major role is that in the biblical story of Joseph, where they are presented in the form of a *coat* – a garment, I hasten to add, having no more substance in real life than Cinderella's slipper. This coat was given to Joseph by his *Father* (subconscious) and is therefore an allegorical expression of initiateship, the wearing of these colours being a sign of the accomplished process. Comprehension of this truth will help to explain the rather presumptuous dream experienced by Joseph (Gen. 37; 9) soon after taking possession of the many coloured coat, in which he saw the sun, moon and eleven stars making obeisence to him. Ordinarily, one would expect the stars to number twelve, they being alternative signia for the twelve signs of the zodiac (indicative of the mental process), but only eleven are mentioned, the reader thus being left to conclude correctly that Joseph himself is the missing 'star' – the new initiate arrival.

Only a few centuries after this example of Egypto-Babylonian allegory was in current favour, the Greek philosophers of about

400 B.C. applied the Hermetic colours in a different way, aligning them with the pigments used by real life artists in connection with an invention called the Kerotakis – a painter's palette. Artists of that early period used a mixture of pigment and melted wax, and in order to keep the colours workable, it was necessary to keep them warm enough so that the wax did not harden. The Kerotakis, a metal plate on which the colours were held, was kept warm, but not too hot, by placing it over a slow charcoal fire. The Hermeticists immediately seized on this operation as a ready made analogy of their mental work – the *colours* (stages of the process) being applied by means of a *gentle heat* (meditation). Not unexpectedly, the allegorical idea of Joseph's many-coloured coat was further related to the process of dyeing textiles such as the silks mentioned by Karl, for the concept of fixing colours in the material operation is easily analogous to the Hermetic *fixing of colours* (completing the stages), especially if the added factor of mordanting is considered. Before the advent of artificial colouring, natural dyes were used, such as indigo, logwood, fustic, cochineal, Persian berries, orchil, cudbear and cutch. With the exception of indigo and orchil, the dyes applied to textiles were only successful if the fibres of the material had been steeped in mineral salts, a process called mordanting. Apart from the Hermetically suggestive phrase 'mineral salts', further analogy with the mental work could be seen in the general scheme of mordanting, for the process was also used to *fix gold leaf*.

Even the operation to tan skins contained all the ingredients for a ready made allegory. In the era under discussion, the Greek philosophers utilised the oak tree as a prime symbol of the conscious mind, possibly because these great trees were often *hollow* inside, thus being an ideal place in which to conceal *treasure*. The *Golden Fleece* of Jason was hung on an oak tree, and later, Philalethes described how Cadmus was required to *pierce* *Python*, the serpent, through and through against the oak tree.

The process of tanning and its obscure relation to the Hermetic work is explained if one remembers that the skins are treated in an operation which employs the *acid* (the philosophers' VITRIOL) content of oak bark, or *gall*-nuts, in order to bring about a colouring, or *conversion*.

Hence, the whole range of accomplishments accredited by Karl to his guest contained a double meaning perceptible to the

Hermeticist – even to the removal of *odour* from artists' oils, for within the variety of epithets commonly applicable to the conscious mind we can include *dung-heap*. When such a dung-heap is cleaned up, or *purified*, then obviously the *odour* (evil, uncontrolled thoughts) will disappear.

The real message conveyed by Karl's letter is that St Germain was indeed the high initiate he was reputed to be, and that he was good enough to instruct the writer in the procedure of Hermetic transmutation. The literal text, however, remained to confound those not versed in the allegorical code, thus fuelling the improbable mythology which adhered to the St Germain biography.

The preposterous rumour that the Comte knew how to manufacture diamonds is likely to have its origin in a deliberate choice of phrase employed by St Germain himself in one of his communications to a brother Rosicrucian. In 'Le Memorial d'un Mondain', the reminiscences of Count Joseph Maximilian von Lamberg, at one time Chamberlain to the Emperor Joseph II, the author quotes a letter received by him from St Germain, in which the Comte states:

> I am indebted for my knowledge of melting jewels to my second journey to India, in the year 1755, with General Clive, who was under Vice Admiral Watson. On my first journey I had only a very faint idea of the wonderful secret of which we are speaking;

I do not attempt here to vouch for the accuracy of the Comte's claim to have accompanied Clive to India, except to say that the date is right, and that only investigation of the surviving Clive Papers of the East India Company would show if our subject did indeed travel with the expedition, either as St Germain or under one of his many aliases. More importantly, I wish to draw attention to the phrase 'knowledge of melting jewels', upon which the uninformed have seized and enlarged to the point of absurdity. To resolve this misinterpretation, I ask readers to recall a quaint item of folk lore, prevalent in the 12th century, which encouraged the belief that toads carried a precious gemstone hidden inside the skull. Doubtless a succession of luckless toads were consigned to an early end in attempts to prove the truth of the story, but quite understandably, no such biological wonder ever manifested, either in the 12th century or at any other time. The story is, as one can guess, an example of Hermetic myth very much on the lines of the pearl and the oyster, with the toad – a creature that is *black, ugly,* and with *warts* – representing the conscious mind, while the imaginary gemstone plays the part of the pure consciousness – the Philosophers' Stone. Thus the *pearl* symbol is sometimes replaced by a natural gemstone such as a *diamond*.

Returning now to the words of St Germain, it becomes easier to see that when he claims knowledge of 'melting jewels' (with *heat*), or of 'manufacturing diamonds', he is inferring that he has achieved the ability to draw upon the power of his own subconscious, not that he has discovered some technological process capable of rendering crystallised carbon into a molten liquid.

A relevant episode is to be found in the memoirs of a Madame du Hausset, one of the ladies in waiting at the court of Louis 15th. In 1757, St Germain returned to Paris and was at once welcomed back to Versailles and the intimate parties held by the king and Madame Pompadour. One day, Madame Hausset relates, the king showed St Germain a flawed diamond, pointing out dejectedly that it would be worth nearly twice as much were it not for the flaw. Perhaps, he suggested, the Comte, who had so much experience in the manufacture of diamonds, could remove the troublesome flaw? St Germain examined the gem attentively and then agreed, saying that he would return it in one month. Sure enough, at the appointed time, St Germain reappeared at the court and presented the diamond to the king, who saw at once that the flaw had been completely removed. In a transport of delight, Louis immediately weighed the stone, observing that it had only diminished but a little. The monarch was considerably impressed, and notwithstanding the gem was now worth a good deal more than before, would not part with it, but kept it as a curiosity.

Assuming the story to be a true account, very little effort of deduction is required to conclude that the Comte had merely taken the time to find and substitute a flawless diamond of roughly the same size, putting down the loss as an investment in royal goodwill, for St Germain was well able to afford such a gesture. But the more pertinent aspect of this story is the report by Madame Hausset that the king, after expressing great surprise, surmised that the Comte must be worth millions, especially if, as the rumour had it, he possessed the secret of making big diamonds out of little ones. Madame Hausset continues:

> The Comte neither said that he could or could not, but positively asserted that he *knew how to make pearls grow*, and give them the *finest water*.

Here again, from the most unexpected quarter, we find a blatant Hermetic phrase, although quite acceptable if the author was repeating the Comte's words verbatim. The process in which *pearls are made to grow* is, as you now know, the mental work – the *finest water* being just another allegorical name for meditation.

There are, it must be obvious, several more wild stories about St Germain which are open to resolution by the same method, but having made my point that he was in possession of high Hermetic knowledge, and that he and his associates did not hesitate to make use of the allegory pertaining to it, I would rather move on to rationalise not only the Comte's longevity, but also the suggestion that he magically materialised at the centre of political events, no matter where they unexpectedly took place. Any sense of the supernatural with regard to the latter can be quickly dispelled by the recollection that St Germain was a Rosicrucian of high standing, and as such was in close communication with the Grand Masters of many lodges, not only of the Rosicrucian movement itself, but of the Freemasons, Templars, Illuminates, Knights of St John and many other secret organisations. The behind-the-scenes role played by these societies is no figment of the imagination and you will not be unaware that in Governments of modern times, influence upon certain situations is brought to bear by Freemasons who happen to be elected members of Parliament, and by whom the wishes of brother Freemasons will be given priority over those of unaffiliated constituents. The Comte de St Germain, a wealthy man with a powerful family in his background, made an ideal representative of Freemason and Rosicrucian ideals – politically speaking. It is hardly surprising, therefore, to find him acting in the capacity of unofficial and sometimes secret ambassador, as he did for the king of France in the negotiation of a peace treaty with

Prussia in 1760, doing so only because Louis was unable to fully trust his own minister.

As a Rosicrucian of great influence, St Germain would have been offered fraternal access to all European cabinet ministers and would undoubtedly have been privy to much knowledge concerning impending political events, making his appearance at such locations and times no mystery at all. It is only fair to add, however, that during his lifetime, the Comte was known to have travelled under more than a dozen different names, this factor alone accounting for much of the air of intrigue which seems to surround his legend today.

The imaginative hearsays regarding the Comte's supposedly phenomenal longevity have an equally rational explanation and by far the best starting point from which this mystery may be unravelled is a letter penned by a member of the German aristocracy of the period, Prince Karl of Hesse-Cassel, himself a noted Freemason. It was with Prince Karl, at his home in Cassel, that the elderly St Germain lodged during the last years of his life, and Karl states

> He told me he was eighty-eight years of age when he came here . . .

As near as can be determined from the piecemeal history left to us, St Germain became a guest of Prince Karl on a regular basis at some time in 1781, and we can couple this information with evidence supplied by author Louis Bobe in his book, 'Johan Caspar Lavater's Rejse til Danmark i Sommeren' (Copenhagen 1898), wherein he quotes a passage from the church register of the little town of Eckernforde, showing that

> . . . St Germain died on February 27th, 1784 in this town in whose church he was entombed quite privately on March 2nd.

This information is corroborated by the official records of Eckernforde Council in an obligatory legal notice concerning St Germain's estate, an announcement made because the Comte left no will.

Elementary calculations show that if the above information is reliable – and there is no reason to think otherwise – the Comte died at the age of ninety one, a grand span of years but by no means unique. If anything further is to be said on the matter, it must be to add that a number of writers testify to the fact that St Germain never drank alcohol and that he was very much of a vegetarian, a mode of living that may well have appeared eccentric in the eyes of less enlightened contemporaries, but would have certainly contributed towards a long and healthy existence. That, at any rate, is the conclusion reached by Karl of Hesse, who annotated St Germain's devotion to experiments with herbal medicines

> He thoroughly understood herbs and plants and had invented medicines of which he constantly made use and which prolonged his life and health. I still have all his recipes, but the physicians ran riot against his science after his death.

If St Germain's age is thus considered to be satisfactorily established, then the same calculations place his birthdate in the year 1693. We deduce, therefore, that if the rather doubtful incident involving Madame von Georgy took place in reality, the Comte would actually have been fifty years of age in 1743. But we are also required to concede that if the composer, Rameau, had known St Germain at Venice in 1710, the latter would have been a young man of seventeen, rather too early, it may be thought, for him to have become the Hermetic initiate indicated by Rameau's use of the appropriate code phrase, 'a man of fifty'. To resolve this, it is necessary to delve as far as historical data permits into the circumstances of the Comte's birth, and the unfortunate events which befell his family at the time.

Valuable information in Prince Karl's writings helped Isabel Cooper-Oakley successfully to outline the probable history of St Germain's entry into the world, beginning with the disclosure that he was the son of Francis Leopold Ragotzy of Siebenburgen, Transylvania. Political turmoil of the late 17th century had involved the old Prince Francis, St Germain's grandfather, in a losing battle with an Austrian Empire that was expanding rapidly at the instigation of the Catholic Church hierarchy. The old Prince Francis lost his life in the struggle and thus his son, the Comte's father, was brought up under the care of the Austrian

Court at Vienna. When he eventually came of age, the Emperor handed back some of the confiscated properties, albeit conditional on the observance of many restrictions, and so Francis Leopold was able to set up his own home and enter into marriage with Charlotte Amelia, a daughter of the Hesse-Wahnfried line. Records state that the wedding took place in 1694, and that there were three children, boys Joseph and George, and one girl named after her mother. Although no more is heard of the girl, the destinies of the two sons are chronicled, one continuing an unsuccessful struggle against the authority of the Austrian court until his eventual death, the other living quietly in Vienna and apparently on good terms with the Emperor. The same records, however, show a copy of Francis Leopold's will, in which is mentioned a third son, apparently not from the union with Charlotte Amelia.

It is Prince Karl of Hesse who provides an explanation for this minor mystery, stating that St Germain himself admitted to being the son of Prince Ragotzy of Transylvania *by his first wife*, a Tekeli (family name of the Graf Tekeli who married the Comte's widowed grandmother). The circumstances of this first marriage and its end remain a mystery simply because information relating to it has not survived. But – and again from the Comte's own lips – we are informed that while still very young, St Germain was placed in the care of Gian Gastone, the last Grand Duke of Tuscany, who saw to his upbringing and sent him to the University of Siena to be educated. And in this morsel of personal history lies the key to the Comte's early acquisition of Hermetic knowledge. Gian Gastone was a Medici, and the House of Medici, once the ruling family of all Florence, was possessor and guardian of the Gnostic truth, revealing it only to those few who were so qualified to receive it. As Prince Karl points out:

> This House (Medici), as is well known, was in possession of the highest possible knowledge, and it is not surprising that he should have drawn his earlier knowledge from them . . .

The 'highest possible knowledge' mentioned here is the same as that of the Plantagenets, Hermetic *understanding*. St Germain's true name, therefore, was Ragotzy (or Ragoczy – there are some permutations of the spelling according to each neighbouring province), and no doubt there is keen interest to know why and in what circumstance the Comte chose the pseudonym by which he was so well recognised. For the answer, we return to the Ragotzy family history, at the time of Francis Leopold's marriage to Charlotte Amelia. No sooner had Francis, St Germain's father, been reinstated as head of his former province of Siebenburgen than he began to conspire with his noblemen against the Austrians with the object of regaining his family's independence. But his plots failed and all his properties were annexed – this time for good. A furious Austrian Emperor demanded that his two sons by Charlotte Amelia renounce entirely the name of Ragotzy, forcing them to accept instead the titles of St Carlo and St Elizabeth. According to Prince Karl of Hesse, from information gathered in conversations with his guest, when the Comte heard of the new titles, he said to himself:

> Very well, I will call myself Sanctus Germano, the Holy Brother.

To appreciate the reason why such an appellation was selected we must consult Hermetic symbolism – not for 'Germano', which does indeed mean 'brother' and in Old French would be translated as 'Germain'. But why 'Sanctus'?

In the Early and Middle Ages, it was the custom of the initiates upon attaining a certain level of understanding to adopt a Latinized version of their name, thus signifying the achievement. Hence Robert Fludd, the English Alchemist and Grand Master of the Priory of Sion, became Robertus Fluctibus, while Theophrastus von Hohenheim signed his writings with the name Paracelsus. This practice was already old even in the 16th century and can be traced back to the time when the Gospels were titled. Matthew, Mark, Luke and John, the four names to whom the texts are attributed, were high initiates of the mental work, as the allegorical content of their writing indisputably shows. As everyone is well aware, they are listed in the New Testament as *Saint* Matthew, *Saint* Mark, *Saint* Luke and *Saint* John. Whatever you have come to believe regarding this prefix, the inner meaning of *Saint* as applied by the Hermetic writer simply shows that the man whose name it precedes was versed in the hidden science of Gnosticism. And when Prince Ragotzy adopted the name *Saint Germain*, he was proclaiming the same achievement.

The testimony of the Comte himself indicates that he attained a high degree of initiateship only after his second journey to India in 1755, at which date he would have been sixty two years old – a fragment of information that allows us to appreciate how long the mental work must be continued before the highest state can be reached. And some measure of the Comte's advance along the Hermetic path may be gained from an unusual statement made to the Prussian Ambassador in Dresden, in 1777:

> I hold nature in my hands, and in the same way that God created the world, so too I can conjure forth everything I wish from the void.

To many, this has appeared as arrogant, or even blasphemous, but behind this statement rests one of the more important Hermetic truths, available only to those who have developed the power of understanding capable of knowing it. Franz Hartmann echoes the same mystical principle when he says:

> If we could hold on to a thought, we would be able to create. But who but the enlightened can hold on to a thought?

As a final statement on St Germain the initiate, and in reference to his accredited wealth, I point out that in keeping with his aristocratic status as a provincial Prince, his adopted House of Medici made adequate arrangements for funds sufficient to last him all his life. But these arrangements were a private affair, and hence to all others, a 'mystery'.

Chapter Nine

Daniel Defoe

The 18th and 19th centuries saw the gradual emergence of popular dramatic and romantic fiction, the precursors of today's action and glamour novel. This much is common knowledge, but what the greater mass of readership may not realise is that the art of allegorising the mental process was the motivating force behind many of those works now regarded as classics, including *Gulliver's Travels*, the original *Frankenstein*, *Robinson Crusoe* and even Rider Haggard's famous *She*.

The late 1600s, an epoch of piracy on the high seas, of the first treasure cache on the famed Cocos Island, and continued exploration of the vast South Americas, provided material and incentive enough for Daniel Defoe's first full length novel, *Robinson Crusoe*, the plot of which was based upon true circumstances which befell a Scottish sailor in 1704. After challenging the authority of his captain, deckhand Alexander Selkirk was left ashore on one of the Juan Fernandez Islands, located about 350 miles off Valparasio and the coast of Chile. Selkirk was marooned for a little over four years before being picked up by a privateer under the command of Captain Woodes-Rogers. The Captain's account of the rescue appeared in print in 1712, telling how he found Selkirk, who by then could only speak his own language with the greatest difficulty, his listeners barely able to understand the half-formed words. He was dressed in goatskins and his bare feet were so hardened that he was unable to resume wearing shoes without his feet swelling. At first, when left alone on the uninhabited island, he suffered terrible melancholy, but in time overcame this. Later on, he was able to tame some of the wild cats which, according to the account, would lie about him in their hundreds.

The narrative created immediate interest and was seized upon by Defoe as an ideal vehicle for an allegory of the process, the circumstances of the plot being ready-made to carry existing code words. Many less informed commentators have remarked wonderingly upon the obvious allegorical nature of the story, among them Karl Marx who, at a loss to interpret it correctly, sneered in particular at its religious content. Others have commented at length on Defoe's ideas regarding imports and exports, the analysis of human labour and, especially, the puzzling quality of money. This only has value when used in trade but dazzles men into thinking it has an intrinsic value. This latter theme, perhaps those commentators were aware, is an echo of Thomas More's *Utopia*, the inhabitants of which no longer place any importance on money.

> And who does not see that fraud, theft, robberies, quarrels, tumult, contentions, seditions, murders, treacheries and witchcrafts, that are indeed rather punished than restrained by the severities of the law, would fall off if money were not more valued by the world. Men's fears, solicitudes, cares labours and watchings would all perish in the same moment that the value of money did sink. Even poverty itself, for the relief of which money seems most necessary, would fall if there were no more money in the world.
>
> (*Utopia* Thomas More)

This theme, as is well known, is one of the basic tenets of Communism, but one which can never be successfully applied because, as only the Hermeticists seem to be able to grasp, it is not simply money that is the 'root of all evil', but Man's inherent greed and avariciousness, inbred into the outward personality. Thus, the panacea which all Communists so earnestly seek will never be found unless all participants are Hermetically enlightened, or at least have proceeded far enough along the Hermetic path for the words of More and Defoe to appear as more than wishful thinking.

As for Defoe's religious views, it is known that he was of an unorthodox frame of mind, and this is most certainly borne out by the ideas found in the text of *Robinson Crusoe*.

The Hermetic clues and code words in this classic tale are so prolific that to attempt to cover them all would be unrealistic, and also, in terms of the space required, detrimental to the expositions which follow. I therefore intend to encapsulate the story, touching on the outstanding Hermetic passages as they occur, and drawing attention to the hidden content by means of the usual emphasis.

The first and most obvious clue lies two-fold in the name of the central character, *Robin*son *Crusoe*, the latter half being easier to interpret, due to its association with biblical symbolism. 'Crusoe' is an anglicized version of 'kreutznaer', 'kreutz' being the German for 'cross'. Also, 'Crusoe' is very close to the Latin 'crucis' (*cross*), both these similarities leaving the reader in no doubt that 'Crusoe' is meant to represent someone connected with the biblical *cross* (i.e., the mental process). This conclusion is confirmed when we find that he is a *third son*, and that he yearns to embark upon a *voyage*, a *quest* for adventure, against the wishes of his family (showing that his ideas are contrary to those of the majority). To this end, Crusoe *boards a ship* bound for London (begins the process), but it runs into a fierce *storm* (upheaval in the mind). Crusoe is sick and regrets his impetuosity, saying

> . . . I resolved that I would, like a *true prodigal son, go home to my father* . . .

With incomplete knowledge of Hermetic allegory, it might be thought that Crusoe was preparing to abandon the process only just begun, but the true interpretation lies with the New Testament story of the Prodigal Son, to which the line above so clearly refers. This myth, peculiar to Luke, chapter 15, and familiar to Hemeticists, portrays the conscious mind as a son dissipating his time and energy in outward living, but eventually returning to his *Father* (God, the subconscious) by means of the mental process, at the accomplishment of which, the son is *dressed in a fine robe* (verse 22) just like Joseph's many-coloured coat.

Despite his experience, Crusoe boards another ship, this time bound for *Africa*, where he soon runs foul of slave traders and is taken prisoner. He manages to give them the slip, thus making his *escape from slavery* (attaining the right form of thinking that will allow him to accomplish the process). Other adventures follow, including the sighting of a *monster lion*, which he *plans to kill* (the 'monster lion' being the semi-initiated conscious mind which must be subjugated, or 'killed'). This task requires him to carry *three* guns and to use *three* bullets (bullets are made of *lead*, symbol of the conscious mind) to bring about the lion's eventual despatch. Crusoe then *skins the lion* (analogy from Roman times for the completion of the mental work – see the period figure of Hercules with a lion's pelt over one arm). It is made quite clear to the reader that Crusoe ends this part of his saga with a *lion's* skin, the skin of a *leopard* (with its spots), and a lump of *beeswax*.

As you will have likely begun to appreciate, virtually every page of Defoe's text contains a carefully hidden allegorical phrase, referring by means of long established code words to the mental work, and thus it continues throughout the whole of the book. I don't doubt that many will be unable to accept this assertion, their scepticism prevailing where understanding and insight is lacking. I ask the doubters, however, to ponder on a single aspect of the expositions so far. In the context of an adventure in Africa, Defoe's description of the slaying of a 'monster lion' does not seem out of place, despite the rather curious stipulation of three guns and three shots. In fact, it reads as quite a natural sequence. But a few paragraphs later, Crusoe is made to kill another 'monster', this time a leopard. Apart from the anticlimatic impression created by the repetition, Defoe's description of this second action is, to say the least, noticably half-hearted, leaving even the most generous critic to wonder why on earth the sequence was retained in publication. The reader may, of course, accuse Defoe and his editor of sheer lack of literary expertise. On the other hand, I know from personal research that the 'leopard' symbol is to be found applied in exactly the same way in Alchemical manuscripts that the average reader would not dream of studying. The inference is, therefore, that Defoe wrote the sequence in with a definite purpose in mind although what that purpose may be is left to the perspicacity of the reader.

Continuing with the text, Crusoe is eventually made to encounter the *storm* which casts him ashore on a remote uninhabited island somewhere in Carribean waters. It is at this point that Defoe exhibits an allegorical construction which differs in an extremely subtle way from the expected. Unlike the stories of Zoroaster, Jesus, or Apollonius, where the central character personifies an enlightened conscious mind proceeding towards an amalgamation with the subconscious, Crusoe is now seen as representing the concealed spark of subconscious Essence within us all. To explain simply: the birth of every animate being is only achieved because a spark of pure consciousness, the

Essence, is attracted into the physical to provide sentience for the duration of earthly sojourn. This spark remains undetected by the outer senses unless the effort of the Hermetic process is undertaken, and when physical death occurs, the spark of Essence returns once more to the whole, that which has been called the Universal Mind, or the One. Quite cleverly, therefore, Defoe has inverted the usual presentation of Hermetic allegory by having Crusoe (personifying the spark of Essence, i.e., the subconscious) cast away on a deserted island (now separated from the One by being incarcerated within an animate being). At the same time, he does not depart from the familiar collection of code words used by all initiate writers.

Consolidating his position on the island, Crusoe selects a *hollow in a rock* (the *cave* of the inner mind where the subconscious resides) and proceeds to build a *fortress* around it (isolation of the subconscious from the conscious mind). Entry into the fortress is difficult, for there is no door. Instead, a *ladder* is used (Jacob's Ladder, i.e. the process).

In time, Crusoe names the cave his 'kitchin' (kitchen – the place where *heat* is used for *cooking*), and we are told that time, *labour* and a great deal of *patience* was exercised as he *built up his house* and *enlarged his cave* (all words and phrases indicating that the process is being carried out). At a loss for a candle, Crusoe makes use of tallow from a goat he killed (sacrifice), which gives him *for the first time a light in his cave* (the first light in the mind, the first glimmerings of exceptional understanding). A small *green* bag is found, once containing corn, but now holding only a few husks which he decides to plant. Green is the traditional colour of initiation, that is, the first revelation in the mind which shows the neophyte how he should proceed into contemplation. It is no surprise, therefore, that the bag once held *corn*, a symbol of meditation in ancient Egypt. In the Bible, this symbolism is extended to *ears of wheat*. Defoe takes it one step further, for his crop turns out to be *barley*. The meaning, though, is identical: he has *planted his first seed* and it is growing (the process is under way).

As time passes, Crusoe explores the rest of the island, acquiring in his adventure a tame parrot which he teaches to *speak his name*. In allegory, birds are used to signify the inner spirit in the same way that animals represent the conscious mind. The

Eagle is a symbol of initiation, the Pelican a Rosicrucian emblem of the whole process. Noah, you may recall, sent out first from the Ark a Raven, which is a *black* bird, and then on *three* occasions, a Dove, which is *white*. Crusoe's parrot, however, being a close associate of the Essence (represented by Crusoe) is an exotic bird and therefore *multi-coloured*, just like Joseph's *coat*.

Later in the narrative, this parrot is made to wake Crusoe from a *profound sleep* by calling; 'Robin, Robin, Robin Crusoe!'. According to Robert Graves, an author recognised for his penetrating research into folk lore and symbolism, the name 'Robin' is associated with the zodiacal sign of the *Ram* (Aries – emblem of concentrative power), and also with the *Devil*. From Ernest Scott (*People of the Secret*) comes the Persian equivalent, 'Rah-bin' ('he who sees the road', or one who knows how to accomplish the process). These two sources alone show the name to be representative of the conscious mind in the course of the process. And you will note that the parrot calls the name *three* times.

Possibly the most memorable event in the Crusoe saga is his discovery of a single footprint in the sand. He is *thunderstruck*, because the sand shows no impression other than the solitary print, a fact which defies rational explanation. The Hermetic answer, however, is remarkably simple. Crusoe, as a representative of the subconscious 'castaway' in the physical body, receives the first sign (the footprint) that an attempt to make contact is being made by the conscious mind, here characterised by Friday, who is *dark*-skinned (same as *black*). Confirmation that this interpretation is correct comes when Crusoe attributes the footprint to the *work of the Devil* (the mental work going on in the conscious mind).

Before Friday makes his appearance, the text contains some important paragraphs in which Crusoe explores the idea of intuition, a phenomenon which he calls 'secret hints'. In a lengthy and somewhat torturous passage, he muses to himself, recalling instances in life where danger threatened, but from which deliverance came, seemingly by chance and often without his being aware of it.

> . . . when sense, our own inclination, and perhaps business has called to go the other way, yet a strange impression on the mind, from we know not what springs, and by we

know not what power, shall over-rule us to go this way; and it shall afterwards appear that had we gone that way which we should have gone, and even to our imagination should have gone, we should have been ruined. . . .

Defoe is here conveying the truth that the intuition is an aspect of the pure consciousness that develops in the realm of the conscious mind as the process is carried out.

One day Crusoe became aware that cannibals were ashore on the other side of the island and he *climbed a hill* to see what was happening. There were *thirty* (containing the number *three*) natives dancing *in a circle* (reversal of thoughts) round a *cooking fire*, and even as Crusoe *watched* (biblical term for meditation), one of their intended victims seized a chance to escape, *running* towards the hill on which Crusoe stood. *Three* cannibals pursue the fugitive, but one gave up the chase because he didn't want to *cross water* (did not believe in the process and gave it up). The other two were *killed*, one by Crusoe, the other by the fugitive himself.

Quite aside from the clues I have indicated, insight into this passage will reveal the 'cannibals' to be, like the 'vampires', the general mass of people who are unaware of the possibilities offered by their own minds, the orthodox thinkers. The fugitive represents the small minority who break away (make their escape) from the accepted mode of erroneous religious thought and by doing so, discover the truth. In this passage, the fugitive makes this getaway by *running*, a physical exercise meant to portray the effort involved in application of the mental work, just as in other texts it is symbolised by a *combat*, or the *ascent of a mountain*. It is noticable, too, that the fugitive runs towards the hill on which Crusoe is hiding (the escaper turns towards the place where the subconscious is concealed).

The fugitive is grateful and exceedingly *impressed by Crusoe's power to kill* at a distance with a gun. To show his complete obesience to the *white* man's authority, he *kneels* before him and with his head touching the floor. Then he *takes Crusoe's foot in his hand and places it atop his own head*. This is a most ancient and important piece of symbolism and I leave interpretation to the 19th century adept, Eliphas Levi, as quoted in his *Dogme et Ritual de la Haute Magie*:

> The sovereign will (of the adept) is represented in our
> symbols by the Woman who crushes the Serpent's head,
> and by the resplendent Angel who represses the Dragon,
> and holds him under his foot and spear.

Thus, the fugitive's action represents not a physical subjugation, but a mental one, a successful act of reflection where the
initiate has at last managed to control his thoughts. Crusoe's new
companion makes this gesture several times thereafter.

Crusoe chooses the name 'Friday', an appellation supposedly
to have no other significance but with the day of the week, but if
Babylonian lore is consulted – as allegorical writers often did – it
will be found that *Friday* has equal symbolic meaning with the
metal *copper* and the emotions *desire* and *love*. In turn, this trio is
connected to the planet *Venus*, the *green* planet, don't forget. The
whole range of emblems signifies the conscious mind in the act of
meditation, and thus Friday's role in the allegory is confirmed.

Crusoe will not allow Friday to call him by name, but insists
that he use the term '*master*' (Hermetic for the pure consciousness). As Friday's part in the story develops, similar emblems are
invoked in a continual reiteration of the central allegorical theme.
Perhaps the item most worth recording is that which occurs
during a discussion about the Christian religion, which Crusoe
wants Friday to adopt. The castaway has been at great pains to
describe God, the Devil, and the eternal struggle between them,
at which Friday asks the classic question:

> If your God is so powerful, why does he not destroy and kill
> the Devil?

The initiate answer to this is simplicity itself, for the *Devil* (the
conscious mind) must be made to 'kill' itself (in the course of the
process). Defoe cannot, of course, give such an answer because
the explanation would be heretical, so – no doubt with a Mona
Lisa smile on his face – has Crusoe much taken aback, later to
formulate the reply:

> Like you and I, the Devil is preserved so that he may *repent*
> and be pardoned.

Expressed concisely, the definition of that well known biblical
injunction to 'repent' is to 'change one's thinking', normally

assumed to mean 'to feel contrition', or 'to change from past evil'. In the Hermetic sense, the change of thinking required is from outwards to inwards – a *reversal* that will certainly be a change from past *evil*.

Although allegorical situations continue to occur in profusion, I must pass them by and move forward to the point where Crusoe is at last presented with the means of leaving the island for good. This only takes place after a *combat* between Crusoe's party and some mutineers, a struggle which the former wins. Then, preparing to leave, Crusoe changes into his *fine clothes*, which he had been saving for the occasion (the pure consciousness, now seen in its true splendour at the accomplishment of the process, the symbolism being the same as *robe*, or *coat of many colours*). Visiting the captured mutineers, Crusoe offers them a choice of returning to England with him, where they will stand trial, or of staying on the island in the hope of being picked up by a friendly ship. They choose the latter and Crusoe, mindful of how difficult it was for him to eke out a living at the very first, *leaves them instructions* (as the writers of allegory do). Then he returned to England to begin a *new life*, and to find himself the possessor of a considerable *fortune*.

Mary Shelley

Daniel Defoe was sixty years of age at the time his novel was written and published, and was therefore able to draw upon many years of experience as a writer in order to formulate such a masterful example of Hermetic allegory. To suggest that a similar talent was exhibited by a nineteen-year-old girl may strain the credulity, but so the facts present themselves in the case of Mary, wife of the famous poet, Percy Bysse Shelley.

Hardly necessary though it may be, I must point out that the modern, Hollywood-inspired film scenarios of *Frankenstein* bear little or no resemblance to the original story, and therefore the carefully laid allegory in the latter is seldom carried through to the screen. The original draft of *Frankenstein* was conceived during the summer of 1816, whilst Shelley and his wife Mary were living in Geneva. In the introduction to her story, Mary records that she was an avid listener to the many long conversations between her husband and their regular visitor, Lord Byron.

> During one of these, various philosophical doctrines were discussed, and among others the nature and principle of life, and whether there was any possibility of its ever being discovered and communicated.

The subject was pursued on many a subsequent evening, the upshot being that each participant became determined to write a fiction, the foundation of which would rest upon what was known of the principle of life. Of the three attempts, only Mary's work was ever completed and published – and it may be accepted without reservation that both her husband and Lord Byron assisted and instructed her in the art of allegorical writing.

Mary's tale, she admits, was inspired by the Greek myth of the god Prometheus, of which there are two versions. The first, and probably the more familiar, is that related by Aeschylus, where the hero was punished by *Zeus* by being *bound to a rock* because he stole *fire from heaven* and gave it to mortals. The lesser known version, popular in Roman times, characterises Prometheus as a 'plasticator' who is said to have recreated mankind by animating a figure made of clay. Both these myths have a Hermetic foundation, but it is clear that Mary based her story on the second version.

Those commentators unaware of the allegorical nature of her story have speculated on the fact that the exact method by which the monster is animated is not disclosed – but its very omission is a clue. The author has deliberately avoided being explicit since the allegory itself is the vehicle by which that particular information is conveyed. In their attempts to transfer the story from book to screen, film writers have been forced to centre upon a passage in Mary Shelley's introduction, where she describes a dream from which her original concept arose:

> I saw a hideous phantasm of a man stretched out, and then, on the working of some powerful engine, show signs of life, and stir with an uneasy, half-vital motion.

On the strength of this, many an animation sequence has been presented in a setting reminiscent of a high voltage terminal of the

National Grid System – a powerful 'engine' indeed. The writers may perhaps be forgiven for not recalling that the archaic meaning of the word 'engine' was 'ingenuity' – *turn of mind*.

The story is written from the interwoven viewpoints of *three* different characters, thus possibly hinting at the stages of the process. This may seem a tenuous link, but many an alchemical manuscript has been found to be laid out in three separate parts for the same reason.

The opening scene, presented in the form of a series of letters from a Captain Waldron to his sister, finds Waldron (a *sailor*) and his ship leaving the port of *Archangel* and heading, we are told, into the unexplored regions of the far *north*, the *land of eternal light and magnetic influences* (same as the nether regions of the Aeschylus version of Prometheus – the inner mind). Waldron is engaged in a personal *quest to find a passage* through the frozen wastes and although in great trepidation at what he is about to attempt, maintains that there is *something at work in his soul* which drives him on. Thus, in a minor way, the Captain is presented as a would-be adept embarking on the mental work.

About a month out and temporarily entrapped in pack ice, the ship is enveloped by a thick fog (the realisation of ignorance, or the lack of understanding), but when this disperses, the Captain and his crew are able to see far across the vast expanse of ice. To their amazement, they sight a sledge pulled by dogs and moving steadily towards the *north*. Even more astonishing is the creature sitting in the sledge, for he is seen to have the shape of a man but of gigantic stature (the *giant* – the great potential of the hidden subconscious within the conscious mind). They watch until this strange apparition is lost to view.

The next morning they rescue a man who had been *marooned* on a large slab of floating ice, his sledge broken and only *one dog left alive*. Despite his precarious situation, the man refuses to be taken aboard until he is assured that the ship is sailing northwards and will continue to do so. A European, the stranger is obviously suffering a great *melancholy*. He was, he told them, in pursuit of the creature driving the first sledge and indeed, seemed obsessed with the desire to catch up, for he is thereafter seen often on deck, *continually watching for a sign* of his quarry. Previously, the Captain's letters had bemoaned the fact that he was in an isolated place *without a friend*, but with the stranger's arrival, he writes that he is *drawn to* him and is beginning to *love him like a brother*. Concerned with the other's unceasing misery, the Captain begs to be allowed to help until at last the stranger agrees to relate the circumstances which brought him to the ship.

The viewpoint now shifts from Waldron's to that of Victor Frankenstein, for such is the stranger's name, and in doing so, the more familiar part of the tale is arrived at. If you have not guessed already from the clues discussed so far in this book, *Frankenstein* ('franc', Old French for 'true' – 'stein', German for 'stone' – i.e., *True Stone* of the Philosophers) holds the same characterisation as Robinson Crusoe, the subconscious. His *monster*, shortly to appear, is the conscious mind in the act of the mental work, an interpretation that will become more clear as we proceed.

Frankenstein begins his story by saying that in his youth, he had been obsessed with a thirst for knowledge of 'metaphysical secrets', and in pursuance of this, came by chance on some Hermetic volumes. Their contents captivated him and impelled him to begin an earnest search for the legendary Philosophers' Stone. One day, *at his home*, (in his mind) there was a violent *thunderstorm*, the progress of which he watched with curiosity and delight:

> As I stood at the door, on a sudden, I beheld a stream of *fire* issue from an *old and beautiful oak*, which stood about twenty yards from our house; and so soon as the dazzling light vanished, the oak had disappeared, and nothing remained but the blasted stump.

The supposed tempest described here has a familiar ring to it, and we recall that a remarkably similar event was experienced by Robert Boyle. As with Boyle, Frankenstein's 'storm' is that upheaval in the mind as the understanding begins its development under the influence of the process. The old and beautiful oak signifies the conscious mind with its collection of misconceptions, which at the advent of understanding (the stream of fire) is 'blasted' out. Another noteworthy coincidence arises in the fact that Frankenstein's 'storm', like that of Boyle, took place in Geneva, prompting the possibility that the name might hold some Hermetic significance like that of *Jerusalem*. Perhaps it is because there is a well-known *lake* nearby, or because *Mont Blanc* (the *white* mountain) is only about *forty* miles distant.

A cameo presentation of the Hermetic theme follows when Frankenstein relates how he went to University, there to meet two professors who exerted opposite influences on him. The first, a M. Krempe, is described as being of 'repulsive physiognomy and manners' (in other words, he was *ugly*). Strongly decrying the writings of the Hermetic philosophers, he persuaded Frankenstein to abandon his previous deep study of them, and so it is not difficult to see that M. Krempe represents the non-initiate conscious mind which has no knowledge of the Hermetic Science.

The second professor, M. Waldman, whom Frankenstein meets *quite by chance*, influences him to return to his Hermetic studies with renewed vigour. Professor Waldman is described as being

> . . . *about fifty years of age* . . . a few grey hairs covered his temples, but those at the *back of his head* were nearly *black*.

M. Waldman, therefore, is portrayed as an adept in the course of the mental work, the significant figure *fifty* indicating as much.

After prolonged and intense study, Frankenstein discovered an 'astonishing secret'. In his unremitting search for the source of life, he had stumbled on the key, the 'cause of generation and life', and he became *capable of bestowing animation upon lifeless matter*. The deepest Hermetic knowledge is indicated by this sentence, in the same way that St Germain maintained he could 'create', just as God does. I need hardly add that his 'astonishing secret' remains undisclosed to the reader, it being conveyed instead by means of the allegory, which at this point in Mary's story, is just getting into its stride.

With fierce resolve, Frankenstein sets about making a man in his laboratory, a being of gigantic stature, 'that is to say, about eight feet tall'. Contrary to what most film makers would have us believe, the laboratory is not an underground cellar but

> . . . a solitary chamber, or rather cell, at the top of the house. . . .

A cell, as we are all aware, is hardly noted for its generous space and it strikes one as a trifle incongruous to select such a place in which to make an eight foot tall man. But such incongruity is intentional, for this 'cell' at the 'top of the house' indicates the mind (the *laboratory*) where the *experiment* will take place. Comparable symbolism will be found in the Last Supper sequence, previously discussed, where Jesus and his disciples gather in an *upstairs room*. And to further confirm the interpretation, the text has Frankenstein relate that

> . . . the *moon* gazed on my *midnight labours*, while with unrelaxed and breathless eagerness, *I pursued nature to her hiding place*.

When at last the *monster* is animated, it is so repulsive in appearance, so hideous a creature, that Frankenstein cannot bear to look at it and runs forthwith from the house. Undue emphasis seems to have been placed on the creature's ugliness, but it is not only intentional but necessary, showing that in the course of the mental work, the first contact with the pure consciousness experienced by the neophyte will be brief because, as yet, the two minds are still incompatible, and more contemplative work is required. Thus, Frankenstein, the pure consciousness, is made to *run from the house*.

Too wretched to return to his laboratory and face the monster, Frankenstein spends the rest of the night in an open courtyard, where in the morning, he chances to meet Henry Clerval, an old friend of the family who at once remarks on Frankenstein's distraught appearance:

> (you appear) . . . so thin and pale; you look as if you had been *watching* several nights.

This covert reference to meditation ('watching') is accompanied by a reminder that Frankenstein has omitted to write to his family for several months and that they are becoming increasingly worried:

> . . . they *cannot understand your silence*.

This 'silence' is, of course, that which Frankenstein achieved in the mind while he was making his monster (accomplishing the process).

Months later, with the monster having disappeared and its

whereabouts unknown, news arrives that Frankenstein's *younger brother* William has been murdered. At once, Victor returns to his home in Geneva, arriving at the height of a *thunderstorm*, and it is while pausing to *watch* the effects of the storm that he is startled to catch a brief glimpse of the monster (second contact between the conscious mind and the subconscious, signalled by the advent of another mental upheaval, the storm). A close friend of the family, a young girl named Justine, is accused, convicted and subsequently executed for William's murder, at which Frankenstein is devastated, for he knows well enough that the monster is the guilty party, but cannot bring proof without disclosing that he himself is the one who created the creature. Utterly distraught, Victor seeks solace in a long, lonely walk through the mountains, eventually drawing near to the high peak of Mont Blanc (the *white* mountain – near the second stage of the process). Arriving at the top of a nearby peak *at noon* (when the *Sun* is high), he sees the monster approaching.

The text now shifts to the third viewpoint, the story told by the Monster, beginning at its 'birth', when Frankenstein ran from the house. Confused, the creature had wandered from the house and into a nearby *forest*. The expression 'entering the forest', in Hermetic parlance, is analogous to the conscious mind when it enters upon the process of meditation. The forest is *green*, the colour of initiation, and to further confirm Mary Shelley's intent, the text says that at first the Monster was desolate and miserable, until *night* fell and the *moon* rose (state of reflection, or meditation), whereupon he felt a strange fascination and pleasure.

At first, he lived by eating berries, but one day he came upon the embers of a camp fire and was able to *keep it from going out* (began meditation), but lack of food near at hand sent him farther from the fire each day until it eventually went out, leaving him no means of igniting it again (first attempts at meditation unsuccessful).

There follows a long sequence which has no relevance to the main plot, and is of little interest to us, except that it is presented in the form of a separate allegory in which the characters are in folklore style, a beautiful young girl, a youth, and a *blind* man. Leaving interpretation until a more opportune time, we move forward to the rendezvous with Frankenstein at the top of the mountain. Here, a lengthy discussion takes place (third contact –

much longer than those before), in which the creature admits killing William and contriving the evidence which convicted Justine, but he holds Frankenstein responsible, as his creator, for these acts, and demands that a female monster be made so that he may enjoy the solace of a mate. Feeling heavy guilt and compassion for his creation, Frankenstein agrees.

Returning to the narrative from Frankenstein's point of view, the location shifts to London where work has begun on a female counterpart of the Monster. Frankenstein fully intends to keep his promise, but one night the male monster, who has shadowed Victor closely in his travels, shows himself at the window of the laboratory. At the sight of him, Victor suddenly realises the enormity of what he is doing, and on impulse, tears the female to pieces. Demented, and vowing a terrible revenge, the Monster disappears. Later, however, he visits Frankenstein's lodgings where both enter into a long argument over the moral issue of such a creation. Frankenstein is intractable. Furious, the Monster says

> *Remember, I shall be with you on your wedding night!*

This phrase is repeated in the remainder of the narrative in several places, as if seeking to impress the words indelibly on the reader's consciousness.

Victor disposes of the female monster's remains by placing them in a *basket* weighted with *stones* and dropping the basket into the sea, an act which was performed at *night*, at a moment when the *moon* was obscured by shadow so that nearby *fishermen* would not see. Unaccountably, some might think, Victor then falls asleep and the boat drifts into the open sea. Waking at morning's light, the sleeper observes himself to be just off the shores of Ireland.

Events move more rapidly from this point, with Frankenstein coming ashore to find himself accused of a murder perpetrated only a short time beforehand. He is horrified to hear that the victim is his great friend Henry Clerval, and realises that as before, the Monster is responsible. Demented, he falls into a *fever*, but is gradually nursed back to health to be told that the local magistrate has exonerated him from blame with regard to Clerval's death.

Set free, Victor returns to Geneva in order to marry his cousin

Elizabeth, but the period is marred by thoughts of the Monster preying on Victor's mind. Nevertheless, the marriage takes place and the couple journey to a country inn where they are to spend their wedding night. Later that evening, when the *moon is high*, Victor stalks the corridors with a pistol in his hand, for he remembers the Monster's threat and feels his presence close by.

Suddenly, there is a scream from their bedroom, and Victor rushes back to his bride. Too late, he arrives to find that she has suffered the same fate as William and Henry – she has been *strangled*. The moon shines down on her corpse and the Monster is seen grinning at Victor through the open window.

You will note that there have been *three* deaths by *strangulation* at the Monster's own hand, thus signifying the complete stages of the process. This is the reason why the Monster is made to say that he will be with Frankenstein on his wedding night – the *wedding* in question being the 'marriage' between the conscious mind and the subconscious. Admittedly, the idea is symbolised in a rather obscure manner as far as the newcomer to allegory is concerned. However, the Monster's final statement, as you will see, will render it a little clearer.

Frankenstein sets out to wreak his revenge by *killing* the Monster, tracking him tirelessly across the Continent. One *night*, he glimpses his quarry boarding a ship bound for the *Black Sea*, and follows relentlessly as the trail leads ever *north*wards. It is a quest which is long and arduous (representative of the mental work), and at times the Monster leaves him messages, one of which reads

> We have yet to wrestle for our lives; but many a hard and miserable hour must you endure until that period arrives.

Again, this is analogous to the mental process. The 'wrestling' that is to take place can be compared either with the Last Supper, the *final hours* of meditation, or with the older allegory of *Jacob* (the initiate) wrestling with the *Angel* (the subconscious – see Gen. 32; 24). The meaning of all three is identical.

Frankenstein closes on the Monster, but a *violent upheaval* of the ice wrecks his sledge, drowning all but one of his *dogs* and leaving him marooned on an ice floe where he was found by Waldron.

As the allegory enters its closing stages, the viewpoint reverts to that of Captain Waldron and his letters. He writes that his ship is in great danger, lost and surrounded by mountains of ice which threaten to crush it. His crew is demanding that as soon as the ship breaks free of the ice, he must turn south and return to safer waters. The Captain, although reluctant to give up his quest, is undecided, at which Frankenstein makes an impassioned speech to the men, calling on their courage and experience. Still grumbling, they retire to discuss the matter among themselves – all of which is intended to portray the lack of belief at the outcome of the mental work, a trait common to the uninitiated masses. Not unexpectedly, therefore, the crew of Waldron's ship, who personify the uninitiated, insist on the voyage being abandoned, and Frankenstein, although near to death, declares that he will go on alone. But it is not long before he expires.

Later that night, the Captain hears a disturbance in the cabin where Victor's body lies, and on investigation discovers the Monster bending over the corpse. During a long speech of explanation and self-justification, the Monster declares

> Neither yours, nor any man's death is needed to consummate the series of my being and accomplish that which must be done; but *it requires my own.*

So saying he springs through the cabin window and out on to the ice, soon to be lost in the darkness.

Bearing in mind that the *Monster* is the conscious mind in the course of the process, the fact of its death as a requisite becomes quite clear, just as it was laid down in allegories as early as that of Zoroaster. However, I must add that a quirk of Mary Shelley's invention is that there is no obvious *resurrection* as there is in Defoe's work, where Crusoe returns to England to *begin a new life*. Obviously it was felt by the author and her advisors that the allegory was of sufficient worth without the addition of such a sensitive issue.

Chapter Ten

Victor Hugo

According to the Rosicrucian fraternity's own documents, author Victor Hugo assumed office as Grand Master of the Priory of Sion in 1844. He had, however, already distinguished himself to his initiate brothers some thirteen years previously by producing the masterpiece of allegory we know so well, *The Hunchback of Notre Dame*. Set in the Paris of 1482, the book centres around the great Cathedral of Notre Dame, a choice of location that was no idle whim on Hugo's part. As the alchemist, Fulcanelli, has shown in his volume *Le Mystère des Cathédrales*, the great Gothic building with its enigmatic bas-reliefs, carvings and statues, is a veritable allegory in stone, its pictorial code words revealing the Hermetic Science to those lucky enough to comprehend. How fitting, then, that the leading character in Hugo's work, a personified version of the ancient *camel* symbol of biblical times, should have the Cathedral as his home.

Harking back for a moment to the allegories just discussed, some correspondence may have been detected in that each story revolves around the two main characters, the allegorical positions of whom are plain and can be easily identified with the Dualistic theme. *Robinson Crusoe* featured Friday as a representative of the conscious mind, while Crusoe himself personifies the pure consciousness. The same situation is apparent in Mary Shelley's work, where the Monster takes the place of Friday, and Frankenstein plays Crusoe's part.

Victor Hugo now enlarges on this idea, placing the emphasis somewhat differently. The pure consciousness is still represented, this time by the horse soldier, *Phoebus* (alternative Greek mythological name for Apollo, the *sun* god). He is a captain, and thus a *master* of men, and his attire is said to be *brightly coloured* (like Joseph's coat). Unlike Crusoe and Frankenstein, though, his role is diminished to make way for two new characters –

Esmeralda and Dom Claude, the alchemist priest. Of this pair, Esmeralda is the most important as she represents the act of reflection alone, and can thus be allied with the *woman* of Hermetic symbolism, and with her ancient counterpart emblems, Isis, Demeter, and Mary the Virgin. She is a *gypsy*, which infers an occult nature, and her name connects her with the emerald, the *green stone* of initiation.

The alchemist, Dom Claude, otherwise called the *arch*deacon, plays a shadowy ʻpart in the beginning, but becomes more prominent as the drama unfolds. His role is overshadowed by those of Esmeralda and the Hunchback, and therefore the fact that he is a secondary personification of an initiate mind in which the work is being carried out may not be readily appreciated by those unversed in the subtleties of Hermetic allegory. For the final accomplishment of the process, his *death* is necessary, and it duly takes place in a suitably spectacular fashion.

As we know, the most powerful performance is given by Quasimodo, and Victor Hugo takes care to inform his readers that the name of this unhappy misfit is the same as that given to the 15th century Easter Sunday holiday. Thus we are left in no doubt that the hunchback is closely connected to a *resurrection*. Quasimodo himself is described as incredibly misshapen and deformed, with a protruding chest and a hump on his back, the latter evoking memories of Richard the Third to readers of this book. The relation of the *hunchback* symbolism to that of the *camel* has been fully explained already and so I move on to other items of significance, such as the fact that Quasimodo has a small *left* eye, while his *right* eye remains entirely *concealed* beneath a huge *wart*, giving the impression of a cyclops, the one-eyed *monster* of Greek mythology. Thus this unfortunate and *ugly* being is clearly a supreme emblem of the conscious mind in the course of the mental work, a statement totally justified by the additional fact that Quasimodo has *red hair* (and note that this *redness* covers the head, where the mind is housed, the inference being that although the ʻhunchback' personifies an as yet uninitiated conscious mind, the possibility of higher evolution awaits). I add that he is big and incredibly strong and is therefore portrayed as a deformed *giant*. Like Esmeralda, Quasimodo is said to be of *gypsy* birth.

As with the works of Defoe and Mary Shelley, Victor Hugo's

narrative digresses often into smaller allegories, side issues of the larger theme, and space precludes coverage of every single one. I shall therefore concentrate on the central allegorical theme, leaving the rest to be solved by those readers whose interest is sufficiently aroused.

The story opens on the *sixth day* of January (which is our Epiphany); in France of that period, a day on which the Feast of Fools takes place. This pageant may be adequately described as similar to the processions which were part of the ancient Mysteries of Egypt and Greece, for its secret significance can only be recognised by the Hermetically *wise*.

The first event of importance to us is the arrival of Esmeralda, who is seen dancing round a *fire*. She is *beautiful*, with *black* eyes and long *black* hair, and she is accompanied by her constant companion, a little *goat*, the *horns* of which are adorned with *gold*. The *goat* – otherwise Capricorn – is one of the twelve symbols that make up the whole zodiac, which like the disciples of the Gospels, is a collective representation of the conscious mind and its ability to undertake the process. The *goat* is a sure-footed *climber of mountains*, its horns symbolic of the crescent *moon* (the fact that they are adorned with gold having the same meaning as Quasimodo's red hair), and that one which accompanies Esmeralda is said to have a small *grey beard*.

Crowds gathered to elect the Fool's Pope are watching a mystery play (the script of which is in allegorical form), but the late arrival of a Cardinal interrupts the performance to such an extent that it has to be abandoned (ironic parody of Church blundering in Hermetic affairs). Attention is transferred completely when Quasimodo appears and he is forthwith elected Fool's Pope.

Gringoire, author of the mystery play, is disappointed at the abandonment of his work, but is attracted to Esmeralda and feels impelled to follow her into a *labyrinth* of back streets as she makes her way to the Court of Miracles. Gringoire remarks significantly to himself:

> Nothing is more favourable to a state of reverie than to follow a pretty woman without knowing whither she is going. In this *voluntary surrender of one's free will* . . . etc.

With reference to the words in italics, the inner meaning of this passage will be made clear if it is remembered that the *pretty woman* represents the act of reflection.

Whilst following Esmeralda, Gringoire witnesses an attempt by Quasimodo, who is acting under the orders of his *master*, Dom Claude, the alchemist, to capture the girl and take her to the cathedral, but the kidnapping is foiled by the arrival of Phoebus. Quasimodo is taken to the dungeons and Esmeralda continues on her way, still dogged by the attentive Gringoire. This cameo scene represents the search by the alchemist, Dom Claude, for the means by which he may accomplish the Hermetic process – in this case it being Esmeralda, the act of reflection. He directs his conscious mind (Quasimodo) to capture her, but the attempt fails.

The Court of Miracles is a gypsy ghetto which has something of the unreal, or supernatural about it. En route to it, Gringoire becomes *dizzy* and asks himself

> If I am I, are these things real? If these things are real, am I really I?

In this sentence we are required to detect the duality of the self and the Self. Which is the real I?, Gringoire is asking.

The unfortunate playwright falls into the clutches of the gypsies and is forced to perform an initiation rite, but he fails this test and is sentenced to be *hanged*. He is only saved by the arrival of Esmeralda, who takes him for her husband, but it is a marriage that is never consummated (portraying Gringoire as one who discovers the way by which the process may be achieved, but who does not take advantage of it).

Accused of attempting to steal Esmeralda, the hunchback is sentenced to be *flogged* at the pillory, and the scene in which this takes place constitutes an elaborate allegory of the mental labour. The idea of flagellation as descriptive of the mental work is, as I have already had occasion to point out, long established in Hermetic lore and can be traced back as far as ancient Egypt where the sign of the flail was the relevant hieroglyph. In France of the 15th and 16th centuries, the same concept was projected in alternative forms, one of which is the tradition called the Flagellation of the Alleluia where, as Fulcanelli reminds us

> . . . the choirboys energetically whipped their humming tops (*sabots*) down the aisles of the cathedral at Langres . . .

The whipping of Quasimodo is preceded by a detailed description of the pillory, it being depicted as a simple sort of structure consisting of a *cubical* mass of *stone*work some ten feet high and *hollow* within. An upper platform, gained by means of a steep flight of *unhewn steps* called '*the ladder*', gave access to a horizontal *wheel* of solid *oak* to which the victim was bound, on his knees (in the position of humility) and with his arms pinioned. An upright shaft of timber, set in motion by a capstan concealed inside the structure, imparted a *rotary motion* to the wheel:

> . . . which always maintained its horizontal position, thus presenting the face of the culprit successively to each side of the square in turn . . .

With the hunchback *bound to the wheel* (alchemical phrase meaning the undergoing of the process), the official torturer begins, making use of a *black* hour glass containing *red* sand to determine the length of time the flogging would take. His whip, slender and with *white* thongs, is wielded with the *right* arm. Quasimodo took his punishment in *silence*, but when it was over, he cried out for *water*. At first, it was denied him, just as Peter denied Christ, but at the *third* cry, Esmeralda appeared, she being the only one to bring him the water.

In what appears to be an inconsequential digression while Quasimodo is suffering the flogging, the author describes how a *dog* ate a *child's wheaten cake* (another reference to the act of meditation).

As bellringer of Notre Dame, Quasimodo always loved the tremendous *noise* created by the great bells, and in fact it had made him *deaf*. It is noticeable that, after his salvation by the gypsy girl, he becomes less inclined to enjoy the clamour, and later on, when he does begin to ring the bells again, he stops as soon as he sees Esmeralda. In this little cameo, the author projects the fact that reflection (Esmeralda's presence) will eventually exercise control over the thoughts (the mental 'noise' will be stilled).

Both Quasimodo and Dom Claude adore Esmeralda from afar and in one paragraph, they are said to be *watching* her dance from a vantage point in the *north tower* of the cathedral, the *gaze* of the alchemist being *fixed* on the gypsy girl's *head*. But Esmeralda has by this time fallen deeply in love with Phoebus. The Captain attempts to take advantage of this when next they meet,

conducting the adoring girl to a *small room*, but they are followed
by the alchemist, who *watches* as Phoebus begins to make love to
her. Enraged, the alchemist *stabs Phoebus* (indicating successful
meditation, as in pinning the Serpent to the oak) in the back,
kisses Esmeralda before she knows what is happening, and then
flees.

Unable to explain away the wounding of Phoebus, Esmeralda
is arrested and charged with attempting to murder him, being
placed to await trial in a *circular* dungeon called the Question
Chamber (the labyrinth of the inner mind). There are no
windows, and entry is made only through an enormous *iron door*
(signifying concentrated effort in meditation). A glowing
furnace fills the vault with *crimson light*. Brought to this chamber,
Esmeralda at first denies the charge against her, but when
subjected to torture, confesses and is sentenced to be *hanged*. The
execution, planned to take place in front of the great cathedral, is
prevented from being carried out by the intervention of the
hunchback, who dramatically seizes her from the very scaffold
and takes her into the cathedral. Carrying her upwards inside the
building, Quasimodo is seen by the watching crowd to appear on
balconies at *three* different levels, each time crying; 'Sanctuary!'

The hunchback instals the gypsy girl in a *small cell at the top of the
building* and leaves her to recover. The alchemist, meanwhile,
reflects on these events and *tears out his hair* to see if it has turned
white. Later, at *midnight* and under a *crescent moon*, he climbs one of
the towers to be confronted by the sight of Esmeralda, who is
dressed all in *white* and is accompanied by her goat, but he cannot
reach her.

Quasimodo visits the girl regularly, *keeping watch* over her,
even though she cannot bear to look at him (her glance is the other
way – i.e., *reversed*). The hunchback, realising just how *ugly* he is
compared to the girl, offers to *throw himself to his death from one of
the towers* (considers Hermetic 'death'). But Esmeralda has no
thought for any but Phoebus.

The alchemist is in a mounting passion to possess the gypsy girl
and eventually discovers the *key to the red door*, which gives access
to Esmeralda's cell. He goes to her in the dead of *night*, but she
rejects him and cries out to Quasimodo for help. Sleeping
nearby, Quasimodo is roused and rushes in, but as it is *all dark* in
the cell, and as he is *deaf*, he cannot either hear or see that the

intruder is his own master, and so does not heed the command to stop until he has dragged the alchemist out of the cell and into the *moonlight*.

Furious because Esmeralda will not yield to him, Dom Claude appeals to Parliament for a decree to enter the sanctuary within *three* days and take the girl by force to the scaffold, but Esmeralda's gypsy friends set out to rescue her before the prescribed time, by attacking the cathedral in force.

It is worth pausing at this juncture to mention that the author names this band of gypsies the *Argotiers*, the significance of this lying in the fact that the original Argotiers were the *sailors* who helped Jason secure the *Golden Fleece*.

Quasimodo, seeking to repel the attacking force, hurls down a great wooden beam from the cathedral roof, but the gypsies seize upon it to use as a *battering ram* (hieroglyph of the concentrated attention) with which to force open the main doors. In a further effort to drive them off, the hunchback hurls down blocks of *stone* and finally, *molten lead* (lead – i.e., the conscious mind – that has been subjected to the *fire*). One of the gypsy band, more adventurous than the rest, *gains entry to an upper gallery* by means of a *ladder*, whereupon he attempts to *kill* Quasimodo with an *arrow*, but the hunchback seizes his assailant, *tears off his armour*, and throws him to his *death* from the gallery parapet – all of which constitutes another cameo presentation of the Hermetic process.

The alchemist, still desperate to possess Esmeralda, *knows a secret way* to gain access to her cell and, in company with Gringoire, presents himself. The gypsy girl does not at first recognise the alchemist, for he is all dressed in *black*, his face hidden, he *remains silent* in the background while Gringoire does the talking. Persuading the girl to escape with them, they depart by *water*, in a boat across the Seine. Later, when Esmeralda discovers the identity of the shrouded figure of the alchemist, she is given the choice of marriage with him or death by *hanging*. She chooses the latter, calling the alchemist an *assassin*.

Circumstances conspire to leave the girl by a small, cave-like cell under the road, in which is incarcerated an old crone, whom Esmeralda soon discovers to be her long lost *mother* (the 'mother' that gives birth to the 'child', i.e., the conscious mind in the act of successful meditation). Overjoyed, she joins her in the cell, but the king's men discover her and, ignoring the impassioned pleas of the mother, *break down the stones of the cell* and drag them both out. It is dawn and time for the execution, for *the sun is just rising.* Seeing that her pleadings are of no avail, the mother falls at last into a *profound silence* as she and her daughter are dragged to the gibbet. Here, they are torn from each other's embrace so violently that the mother falls and *dies* on the spot, while the hangman carries Esmeralda *up the ladder.*

High above, in the tower of Notre Dame, the alchemist *watches* the execution taking place, not knowing that Quasimodo is standing *quietly* behind him, also *watching.* They see Esmeralda *hanged,* at which Quasimodo, knowing his master to be responsible for her death, steps forward and pushes him from the parapet. Thus, in true Hermetic style, the alchemical death is achieved as Dom Claude *falls from the tower.*

At the last, Quasimodo makes his sad way to the vault in which Esmeralda's corpse is placed and there *dies,* embracing her remains.

I must state once again that, as lengthy as this exposition may seem, it is by no means complete, for Hugo's text is full of digressions into anecdotes, each of which contain their own Hermetic meaning. These diversions take the form of a deliberate *distraction of attention* away from the main action to something seemingly inconsequential. As an example, some reference is made to the Hermetic carvings which actually exist on the portal of Notre Dame, at the time Esmeralda awaits her execution for the first time. The condemned girl stands ready in her place on the scaffold, but the attention of the man in charge is strangely elsewhere:

> One of the vergers was obliged to notify Maitre Charmoule of the fact, who during all this scene, had set himself to study the bas-relief of the great portal, representing according to some, Abraham's sacrifice, according to others the great Alchemical Operation, the sun being typified by the angel, the fire by the fagot and the operation by Abraham. He was with some difficulty withdrawn from this contemplation . . .

If it is recalled that the biblical patriarchs, of which Abraham was one, are representative of the initiate and are not meant to be considered as real persons, the above description of the bas-relief will become clear as a pointer to the mental work. This is why

Hugo directed the reader's attention suddenly away from the main theme and towards something which he knew to hold Hermetic significance.

Another notable example is the description of the room occupied by the Alchemist, Dom Claude. It is said to be gloomy, ill-lit and filled with the paraphernalia expected of a seeker after transmuted gold – skulls, parchments, alembics, compasses and to the *left* of the armchair, a large furnace. But all is neglect, grime and cobwebs, the furnace showing signs of not having been lighted for some considerable time:

> . . . the glass mask, which Jehan noted among the alchemist's tools and which was doubtless used to protect the archdeacon's face when handling any dangerous substance, lay in a corner covered with dust and apparently forgotten. Beside it lay a pair of bellows, equally dusty, the upper side of which bore this motto encrusted in letters of copper 'Spira, spera!' (Blow and hope!).

In this carefully phrased passage, Victor Hugo is inferring that the Alchemist, Dom Claude – who, recall, is personifying a real initiate – once laboured under the misapprehension that the Hermetic work was material, or physical, and that he attempted to perform a chemical transmutation with metals in the hope of making gold. The signs of neglect, however, show that the Alchemist has become wiser, now knowing the process to be one that is performed in the mind alone. Thus, Hugo, in the tradition of all knowing alchemists makes fun of the uninformed, especially by use of the motto 'Spira, spera', in which is concealed a very ironic truth that only the developed understanding can appreciate.

Henry Rider Haggard

Doubtless it seems the height of absurdity to suggest that a text of romantic fiction such as *She* can hold the same allegorical message as the Gospels, the mention of one with the other being near to blasphemy in the eyes of the devout, ecclesiastical scholar. But perhaps those gentlemen of great learning yet little understanding may be excused, for millions have enjoyed

Haggard's imaginative novel without ever suspecting the presence of a carefully contrived inner meaning.

Sir Henry Rider Haggard's biographical details give no hint of Hermetic knowledge, although much emphasis is placed on his consuming interest in Spiritualism, a study which began as early as his eighteenth year. Spiritualism, however, is the poor relation of Hermeticism and youthful interest in the phenomenon in no way accounts for the wealth of allegorical detail woven into the text of *She*.

In 1884, Haggard was a twenty-eight year old lawyer practising at the Temple, in London, already having attempted several romantic novels without much success. One day, while waiting for briefs, he read Robert Louis Stevenson's *Treasure Island*, an experience that at once impelled him to try his hand at adventure stories for boys. The immediate result was a manuscript called *King Solomon's Mines* which, when finally accepted for publication, became his first best seller.

It is necessary to remind the reader here that the very title of Haggard's book is suggestive of allegory, and therefore there may be some truth to the astonishing claim by the author of the Rosicrucian document quoted at the opening of chapter one, that 'inexplicable success' is due to this quality of allegory. I now add that the text of Stevenson's *Treasure Island* contains the same allegory, albeit much restrained compared to the works of Defoe and Hugo. It is known that Stevenson and Haggard communicated, but I need hardly add that any Hermetic ideas that may have been exchanged in their letters would not be perceptible to the general reader.

Six years of Haggard's youth had already been spent in Africa, where he soaked up the lore around which *King Solomon's Mines* was constructed. Doctor Dee, as we have seen, knew only too well how legendary those mines could be. It is also apparent that Haggard steeped himself in the symbolism of the ancient Egyptian Mystery schools, a study that is put to excellent use in *She*.

Stevenson admits to being much influenced by the work of Hugo, and the same appears to be true of Haggard for, as in the text of *The Hunchback of Notre Dame*, he employs four main characters to project the allegory.

The first of these is the *hero* (Greek for initiate), Leo Vincey, described as strong, tall, handsome, and with a *look of power*. His head was covered in a mass of *golden* curls, for which he was likened to the Greek god, *Apollo* (the *Sun*). It is easy to see that Leo is comparable to Hugo's Phoebus (the *sun* of the subconscious), this interpretation being supported by the remarkable choice of name for the character, it being as close as possible to the real life initiate, Leonardo da Vinci. Reinforcing the supposition that this is no idle comparison, Haggard's text makes it clear that the name 'Leo Vincey' is a modern abbreviation of Leo de Vincey, and that Leo's grandfather bore the Christian name of *Lionel* (*Lion – El*, the *SunGod*).

The conscious mind – the hunchback in Hugo's story – is projected in the character Holly, who is about *forty* years of age, *ugly* in features, and *bearded*. In one paragraph, he is made to *look at himself in a mirror* so that he may remark how ugly he is. In another, he is depicted as a woman-hater (does not know the *woman* of reflection), and that because of this the women all call him a *monster*. The name 'Holly' is not without its age-old significance, for it can be allied with the 'bramble', 'thicket', and 'burning bush' symbolism of the Bible, which we have previously touched upon. There is also a possible association with the prickly *crown of thorns*; and don't forget that the holly itself has *red* berries.

Ayesha, as you may easily guess, takes the place of Esmeralda, the *woman* of reflection, for she is called the *Virgin Queen* and is said to be immortal. At her first appearance she is seen to be *wrapped in white* although, like Esmeralda, she has long *black* hair.

The fourth major character is a manservant bearing the name *Job* (again personification of the initiate). Said to be honest and to have a *round face* (circular motion suggested – i.e., reversal of thoughts), Job corresponds to Hugo's alchemist, Dom Claude, in allegorical characterisation.

In a carefully worded prologue, the Hermetic theme of *Beauty* versus the *Beast* (Leo and Holly respectively) is made crystal clear, with the agelessness of the inner meaning being suggested by the fact that Leo's ancestry can be traced back to ancient Egypt. Anyone still in doubt as to the presence of allegory is now referred to a broad hint by the author, who as 'editor', states:

At first I was inclined to believe that this history . . . was some gigantic allegory of which I could not catch the meaning . . .

The adventure proper opens with a flashback in time, when Leo's father visits Holly to entrust him with the care of his only son, and to place in his charge a mysterious iron-bound chest. Thus the *father* entrusts Holly (the conscious mind) with his *son*, an analogy of the spark of pure consciousness being detached from the Universal Mind and incarcerated in a human at the advent of physical birth. The *iron-bound chest* represents the Hermetic mystery, of which few know, the secret being locked up in the recesses of the mind.

Holly accepts the trusteeship and engages a manservant to look after the child. In this way Job makes his entry into the story.

When Leo reaches the age of twenty-five, it is time to open the chest (discover the process) so as to *receive his father's legacy*. *Three* keys are needed, the first being a large, fairly modern key which opens the outer lock. Inside the chest rests a smaller one, ebony *black* and *bound* in every direction with flat bands of *iron*. The second key is of far older design and, upon using it to open the second chest, there is revealed inside a magnificent *silver casket* of Egyptian workmanship and on which are representations of the Sphinx (the Mystery). The third key, unlike anything they have seen before, is fashioned entirely of *silver* (full power of reflection). It is described as being 'a strip of solid silver with a bar placed across to serve as a handle'. Thus it is in the shape of a 'T', or Tau (the Key to the Mysteries). Unlocking the third chest, they discover *three* parchments and an ancient *vase* (the Hermetic vase – man's mind).

The documents relate an incredible story of immortality, which Holly cannot bring himself to believe (being the conscious mind without the inner knowledge and thus a sceptic, he wouldn't), but Leo accepts it as fact and after some discussion the *three* of them, Leo, Holly and Job, set out on a quest, following the directions given on the parchment.

In classical allegories, the entry into the inner mind is depicted as a journey, half of which is on *water*, and half on *land*, but Haggard introduces his own peculiar variation of this piece of established lore by dividing the journey into *three* parts, yet still retaining the dual symbolism. He does this by the simple expedient of making the first segment a voyage on *water*, the second a trek through a *swamp* (a mixture of water and land), and the concluding leg of the journey over *dry land*.

The initial voyage is by now familiar and I only need to add that it was undertaken in a vessel with a *copper* bottom (the metal copper, like the planet Venus, is an emblem belonging to the conscious mind not yet fully initiated). Not surprisingly, there is a *violent storm*, taking place incongruously enough on a *moonlit night*, as a result of which our heros are cast ashore near a great *rock* shaped like a negro's head (the *black* head, or *dead head* of Hermetic tracts – the first stage of the process).

Entering upon the second phase of their journey (second stage of the process), they cross over a swampy morass, encountering much wildlife, some species of which they have never seen before. In particular, there is a goose which has a horn growing out of its skull just between the eyes, and Job is given the honour of naming this remarkable creature the *Unicorn Goose*. Unlike Robinson Crusoe, they do not kill a monster lion, but there is an action packed account of a fierce *combat* between a *lion* and a *crocodile*, the latter being mentioned by Iamblichus as a symbol common to the Egyptian initiates and representative of the semi-initiated conscious mind. The entire account contains a number of unmistakable code phrases and words, as for example at the commencement of the fight, where the crocodile is said to be standing with its front feet on the river bank (*land*) while its hind legs are still in the *water*. In the very next passage, the lion

> . . . roared till the air quivered with the sound, and then with a savage shrieking snarl, *turned round* and clawed hold of the crocodile's *head*. The crocodile shifted his grip, having as we afterwards discovered, *one of its eyes torn out* . . .

The significance of the last sentence is quite plain if we recall that both Mary Shelley's monster and Victor Hugo's hunchback were one-eyed in appearance, but possibly the most lucid interpretation is presented in the Norse Saga telling how Wotan sought a drink from the *fountain* at the roots of the great tree of life. It was guarded by *three* Sybils, who demanded that he surrender one eye in payment. Thereafter, Wotan (personification of an initiate) walked one-eyed through the world, *afire with vision, blind to old allurements*.

The trio's next adventure occurs when they are accosted by

fifty natives, all of whom are dressed in *leopard* skins. These are the People of the Rocks (*stone*), and they take their captives to a *sheltered place* where there are goats and cattle, but *no sheep*. 'Sheep' is the same as the biblical 'lambs', meaning 'thoughts'. This 'sheltered place' therefore, is the quiet mind where all thoughts are stilled by concentrated meditation. In support of this interpretation, there is the additional information that the whole tribe live in a great *cave* in which a *fire continuously burns* (constant meditation). By nature, the natives are cannibalistic, and their head man – a patriarch with a long, *snowy-white beard* – is named Billali. My first impression is that this name is a corruption of the biblical 'Belial', which, while originally indicating 'worthlessness', later became just another name for Satan, the *Devil*. Thus the character Bellali, with his snowy-white beard, seems to represent the conscious mind nearing completion of the mental work. This conclusion is further justified by information given in the very next paragraph which tells of an affinity felt by Bellali for Holly (who is symbolically the same), with the former referring affectionately to Holly by the pet name 'baboon'. This animal also was used by the Egyptians as an emblem of the semi-initiated conscious mind. Haggard, it seems, leaves very little to chance in his allegory, making sure the concealed concept is stated and restated. At the same time, however, he could be tantalisingly obscure, as for instance when he presents a quaint inversion of the Cinderella theme by having Bellali give Holly a perfectly mummified foot as a keepsake.

So far, in their travels from the shore, the trio have been accompanied by an *Arab boatman*, but this unfortunate is now made a human sacrifice by the tribe, an event carried out in the most unusual manner. A *red hot pot is placed over his head*. In describing the scene, Holly remarks

> It's hospitality *turned upside down* . . . In our country we entertain a stranger and give him food to eat. Here, ye eat him and are entertained . . .

Apart from the obvious clue that a *reversal* of the normal is occurring, the tribal cannabalism is brought to the attention, as in *Robinson Crusoe*.

The *third* phase of the journey is now undertaken, this time across *land*. As with previous expositions of full length novels space will not allow me to cover every separate item of coded phraseology as it occurs, and therefore I move on to the point where Ayesha enters the story. She sees Holly first (reflection, being brought into play, has its first effect on the conscious mind). At the time, they are in a *cave*, and she examines him from *behind a veil*. At that moment, the cave is very *silent*, and Holly, *feeling her gaze*, is unaccountably afraid, with beads of *sweat* standing out on his forehead (Rosicrucian 'dew', emblem of the effects of concentrated attention). The *white queen*, as Ayesha is also called, shows Holly a pitcher of water in which she looks to see into the past

. . . this *water* is my *glass* . . . (the 'mirror' of the mind).

She tells Holly that she is two thousand years old (signifying *immortality*) and that she is waiting for her lover to be *born again*. Awe-struck, Holly asks to see her face, persisting with the request despite a warning of the consequences, and when Ayesha *draws aside the veil*, he sees *evil beauty* (successful meditation produces a mixture of the conscious mind, *evil*, and the subconscious, *beauty*).

Later, she shows Holly an enormous pit in which stands a *pyramid of skeletons*, while nearby are to be seen embalmed bodies, *perfectly preserved* (like the body of Christian Rosencreutz in the Rosicrucian Manifestos). Attention is drawn to a pair of the mummies, a man and a woman embracing each other, with an inscription below reading

Wedded in death

Exactly the same sentiment, if you recall, is expressed at the climax of Mary Shelley's novel, where Frankenstein's bride dies on her wedding night at the hands of the Monster.

Offered immortality by Ayesha, the trio follow her towards the inner wall of a *volcano* (a place of *underground fire*), but before proceeding any farther they dispense with the services of the accompanying bearers. It is suggested that Job remain behind also, but he pleads to be allowed to continue with them. Eventually, they agree, and Job is given the somewhat comic duty of carrying a *plank*. The cliff face in front of them appears well nigh unscalable, but Ayesha *shows them a secret way* (indicating the hidden power of meditation). After reaching the top, they are required to traverse a long, winding tunnel which opens out into a mighty cavern. A great wind roars through and ahead of them lies a bottomless pit – the *abyss*. Ayesha says

> Here we must pass . . . be careful lest *giddiness* overcome you . . .

The code word 'giddiness' has the same meaning as 'drunkenness', or 'fever', the interpretation of all three clues having been already given.

To bridge the abyss, they make use of the plank carried by Job – and here I must pause to elaborate on this quaint item of allegorical lore. Many commentators have remarked impatiently upon the tedious description by Daniel Defoe of his hero, Robinson Crusoe, carving a single plank from a felled tree trunk. The labour, being by Crusoe's solitary hand, was long and arduous. It took up a great deal of time with much effort being expended (just like the mental process), and what was even worse was the fact that Crusoe never actually used the finished article. For the purposes of the allegory, however, the fact that he made it at all suffices to carry the hidden message. Rider Haggard, as you now see, employs the same symbolism. The plank carried by Job – and don't forget that he personifies a man undergoing the mental work – is used to *bridge the abyss*. It is therefore analogous of the mental work that must be done in order to bridge that abyss between the conscious mind and the subconscious.

With much trepidation, Haggard's characters cross the abyss, the last being Job himself, who is in such terror that he upsets the plank, allowing it to fall into the depths after he had made the crossing (once having made the transmission of consciousness, there is no going back).

The intrepid party move on, guided by Ayesha, until they reach a *philosopher's cave*, where there once lived a man greatly skilled in the secrets of nature. Ayesha relates how she persuaded him to reveal to her the *secret of the fire* which bestow immortality, and to which they are now going. They pass through *three* successive chambers, the last of which is lit by a soft, unearthly glow, a *rose-coloured light that is beautiful*. It is in this cavern that the fire of immortality appears as a *Cloud*, or *Pilla* (like the Red Sea episode of Moses) of *multi-coloured flame*, which roars forth for the space of *forty* seconds before subsiding, a cycl which is repeated indefinitely. In such close proximity to it, the three men are greatly exhilarated.

On the *third* appearance of the fire, Ayesha steps into the flame, expecting to be renewed with eternal life, but something is wrong. As she returns from the fire, she grows old *before their very eyes*, her hair falling out and her body shrivelling up until it resembles a *small brown monkey*. A little obscure, this, but the overall meaning conveyed is that Ayesha (reflection, and therefore an integral part of the conscious mind which must 'die') is now *dead*, her job being finished at the accomplishment of the process, her connection with the subconscious – the immortal part of the mind – no longer necessary. The sight is so horrific that all three men *feel faint* (dizzy), with Job actually falling down in a fit. When Leo and Holly eventually recover themselves, they are shocked to find that Job is *dead*. It comes as no shock to the initiate reader, however, for as a personification of the initiate mind undergoing the process he must necessarily die, just as Dom Claude died, to comply with the allegorical pattern. Leo fared a little better, for he did not die, but his hair turned *grey* first, and then *white*.

Thus the two survivors of the whole affair retrace their steps to the outside world, after which they return to England, the adventure over. Back home once more, Holly *reflects* on the experience and remarks:

> Often I sit *alone at night,* staring with the *eyes of the mind into the blackness* of unborn time . . .

Such an explicit description of the act of meditation needs no further comment from me. I merely remark – unnecessarily perhaps, at this stage – that in comparing Haggard's allegory with that of Hugo, both symbols of reflection, Ayesha and Esmeralda, are made to die, and so are the operators, Dom Claude and Job. Collectively, they are all representative of man's outer personality and as such, part of the conscious mind. This is why, in both narratives, they die at the same time – Job with Ayesha and the Alchemist with Esmeralda. The fact that both stories are allegorical may explain to modern readers why, unlike most romantic adventures, Phoebus and Leo as the heros do not get the girl in the end.

Chapter Eleven

Conclusion

In the summer of 1983, the *New Statesman* magazine presented a new version of an old interest when it invited readers to attempt the solution of specific problems by way of their dreams. As an example, they were asked to say what is remarkable about the following sentence

> I am not very happy acting pleased whenever prominent scientists overmagnify intellectual enlightenment.

In response, one sixth form pupil wrote in to say that he had experienced the following dream. He was lecturing to a gathering of scientists who were seated at tables scattered about a large hall, but no one was paying any attention to him, at which he became angry and shouted: 'I am not very happy!' The scientists seated at those tables nearest looked up, but at that moment the subject awoke. Recalling the dream, he realised that those who had responded were seated in a peculiar fashion. Only one was at the first table. Two were at the second, three at the third, four at the fourth and five at the fifth. It was then he realised he was being given the answer to the problem, for the sentence begins with a one letter word, moving to two, then to three – and so on up to thirteen. All other correspondents who arrived at the correct answer had experienced dreams that involved counting, with one woman actually dreaming of a Count, that is, a nobleman. But once she realised that the 'count' was a dream pun, she solved the problem.

This foray in search of the subconscious was made at the suggestion of Dr Morton Schatzman, an American psychologist based in London, in the hope that some clue to the apparent purposelessness of the dream world could be discovered. He reminded readers of the many instances where reverie or dream had been known to play an important part in some material discovery, as with the way in which Poincaré described mathematical ideas rising in clouds and dancing before him to collide and combine in the first Fuschian Functions while he lay in bed awaiting sleep, or as with Howe's strange dream which led to the invention of the sewing machine.

Information by way of dreams, Dr Schatzman explained, is elusive simply because it consists mainly of metaphor or puns in imagery. In fact, he concluded, *dreams have their own special language*.

Another of the special problems set for dreamers was the question: Which verb doesn't belong to this particular group?: bring, catch, draw, fight, seek, teach, and think.

One man wrote in to describe an involved dream which featured the actor Michael Caine, who appeared to him and then twice motioned over his shoulder as if at something behind him. On waking, the dreamer recognised the gesture as one seen on the TV panel game *Give Us A Clue*, meaning 'in the past'. And when you put the verbs of the problem in their past tense, all except one rhyme with each other: bought, caught, fought, etc. The odd one out is 'drew'.

The most notable feature of many reported experiences is the fact that a dream entity often appears to know the answer already, as in the examples just quoted, the inevitable conclusion being that part of the dreamer's mind knows the answer even before the dream is experienced. The noted psychologist Carl Jung, a thinker who attained remarkable insight into the subconscious processes, came to the same conclusion and didn't hesitate to say as much:

> For it is only our consciousness that doesn't know; the unconscious seems already informed . . .
>
> (*Man and his Symbols* C. Jung 1964)

The scope of the subconscious answers is by no means limited to mere puns, as the following example clearly shows. Dr Schatzman gave a colleague this question to ponder: which two English words both begin and end with the letters 'he'? The answer is 'headache' and 'heartache'. In his dream, the colleague first experienced an intense pain in his chest. The doctor attending him admitted to knowing what was wrong but refused to say so until the patient confirmed it himself. Goaded by the doctor, the patient said 'I have a coronary'. The doctor testily replied that jargon would not suffice and kept worrying the patient until he eventually used the word 'heartache'. But the pain persisted and the doctor continued to harass him until in exasperation the patient said 'riddles give me a headache'. At this, the dreamer awoke, fully aware of the answers he had given, and as he lay considering these, he recalled that throughout his experience with the dream doctor, various people had been laughing at him in the most peculiar way: 'hee, hee, . . . hee, hee, . . .' Thus the key letters of the problem (HE) were emphasised.

No doubt some correspondence can already be seen between the unreal scenes created by the dream world and the way in which Hermetic writers manipulate symbolism *while in the waking state*, and it suggests that by mastering such allegory one is already treading on the threshold of the subconscious mind.

I make this point in the knowledge that certain readers will view the exposition in this book as inadvertent and meaningless synchronicity, their argument being that if the so-called code words and phrases can be found in one work, they will be present in others chosen at random. To those who hold this opinion, I offer the suggestion that they make their choice of book and start the search for a comparable allegory which will even halfway comply with the terms previously stated. A possible starting point for such an exercise might be *The Lost World*, by Sir Arthur Conan Doyle. This text contains all the potential for such an allegory, it duplicating the main features of *She* – the long journey through hostile territory and wilderness, the climbing of a mountain, monsters, a death, etc. Unfortunately, these possibilities are not utilised by being built into the requisite allegorical framework, and therefore I can authoratively state that if Conan Doyle knew anything of the art, it is not evident in this well known adventure story – nor in any of his famed Sherlock Holmes novels. On the other hand, the story by Robert Louis Stevenson, *Doctor Jekyll and Mister Hyde* offers a wealth of familiar and correctly placed symbolism, the traditional Hermetic theme being visible in the basic Dualist conception, while the process itself indicated with the usual code words and phrases – the whole worked into only a few thousand words.

The decline in spiritual values during the present century is adequately reflected in its literary output, a veritable deluge of meaningless escapism which has all but submerged the art of allegory. The traditional works in which the knowledge is carried are no longer read with care and penetration. Often they are not read at all. And yet Fate decrees that the ancient message may still be delivered on rare occasions, placed before the public's very eyes by way of that supplanter of books, the cinema and television screen. Modern screen writers, in their quest to satisfy the well-nigh insatiable demand for viewing material, sometimes select traditional themes to reproduce as historical or mytho-logical dramatisations. Knowingly or not, unmistakable allegor-ies have been chosen and offered as entertainment. As an example, I quote the 1951 film production of *Pandora and the Flying Dutchman*, starring James Mason and Ava Gardner, a story which in its original form is totally Hermetic, the symbolism being faithfully transferred to the screen.

A second instance, and one which holds a certain mystification, is the 1954 version of *Robinson Crusoe*, directed by Luis Buñuel and featuring Dan O'Herlihy as the castaway. What is so intriguing from our subject's point of view is that while the screen adaptation adhered closely to the original text, certain small sequences were added that were not penned by Defoe – yet they wholly conformed to the long established Hermetic rules. To illustrate: viewers were shown the name of the ship which foundered and cast Crusoe away. It was given as *Gabriel*, which in Hermetic lore is the name of the angel of revelation and thus an indication of the beginning of the mental work. A second example occurs when Crusoe falls into a feverish slumber and dreams of his *father* – and of *water being poured over a pig*. Again this latter act is not to be found in Defoe's text, but is nevertheless authentic, symbolising meditation (*water* being poured) going on in the would-be adept's conscious mind (the *pig*). Of course, additions of this nature could be the result of accidental inspiration on the part of the writer responsible for the film script. If so, these accidents occur on at least five occasions during the film, each time a perfect expression of Hermetic symbolism.

In the 1970s, two other productions in the same category were screened. The first was *The Magic Flute*, starring David Carradine, Eli Wallach and Christopher Lee, where the story line, extracted from authentic Chinese allegorical works, was faithfully reproduced. The second was the BBC2 TV production, *Gawain and the Green Knight*, a transmission of folk lore in which Hermetic allegory is present in every scene.

In my opinion, one of the most delightful screen offerings open to Hermetic study was the 1953 production of *The Captain's Paradise*, with Sir Alec Guinness, Celia Johnson and Yvonne de Carlo in the leading roles. Guinness played the part of a Captain whose ship ferried to and fro between Gibraltar and Kalik, a small port on the North African coast. But the Captain secretly led a double life. In Gibraltar, he maintained a nice home with a quiet, domesticated wife, spending his time there in mundane existence and retiring to bed each night at ten with a cup of cocoa. In stark contrast, his time in the North African port was spent in the company of a young, dark-haired, flashily-dressed mistress, enjoying high living, dancing and drinking, eating out at restaurants every night and roistering until the early hours. In maintaining this dual role, the Captain considered that he had found the key to ideal happiness.

The time came, however, when his wife in Gibraltar became bored and attempted to inject some new interest into their routine by asking to be taken out dancing and to supper. At the same time, the Captain's mistress across the water showed signs of tiring of the high life, favouring instead a more domesticated existence. Deeply disturbed by this trend, the Captain attempted to steer his respective partners back into their original modes of behaviour, and at first it seemed that he had succeeded. But his double life was very nearly exposed when, without his knowledge, his wife decided to pay a sight-seeing visit to Kalik. Whilst there, strolling round the market place, she actually met her husband's mistress and struck up a conversation with her. Neither woman realised the position of the other in respect to the Captain, so no harm was done, but the secretly watching Captain was greatly alarmed.

For a while, all seemed to return to normal, but one night, after bidding his mistress farewell and setting a course for Gibraltar, a boiler room malfunction forced the Captain to put about and return to Kalik. Forced to stay over night while repairs were carried out, he arrived at his mistress's apartment to find her in the act of running away with a local taxi driver. A violent argument between the girl and the taxi driver ensued because she had not told him of her liaison with the Captain. At the height of the quarrel, the Captain walked out – not a moment too soon, for shots rang out and the taxi man was fatally wounded.

Much shaken, the Captain returned to his ship and as soon as it was seaworthy, set off for Gibraltar. Owing to the unexpected delay, he arrived at his home at a time quite out of his normal schedule and surprised his wife just as she was running off with a lover. Stunned, the Captain pleaded with her to stay, but was unable to shake her resolve. Thus, the Captain's 'paradise' was lost forever. Impelled perhaps by conscience, he returned to Kalik to surrender himself to the authorities as the one who killed the taxi driver, thus allowing his mistress a reprieve from impending execution.

In prison, awaiting execution himself, he conceived a brilliant idea. Secretly, he offered a heavy bribe to the firing squad members if they would, at the moment of execution, shoot their officer instead of himself. At their agreement, he made haste to rid himself of all his former possessions and identity, giving his money to his children and his ship to his first officer, and then submitting to the mock execution. After it was over, completely free and with a new identity, he disappeared from public view.

It may be that the strong allegorical content of this story will remain unappreciated until I add emphasis to a few of the many code word clues within the scenario.

The Captain's name was Henry *St James* (the disciple brother of Jesus), he was based at Gibraltar, a place known to all as the 'Rock' (i.e., *stone* – the conscious mind), and the ferry which he commanded was named the *Golden Fleece*, a vessel which plied between two *different lands*. The Captain had two distinct sides to his life (like *Castor* and *Pollux* – the conscious and the sub-conscious). On one side, his *woman* was *quiet and calm*, while on the other, his *mistress* was active and *noisy* – and with this arrangement, the Captain was deluded into believing that he had found perfect happiness (as the non-initiate conscious mind often does). But the situation suddenly began to change (at the advent of spiritual knowledge being gained, a change in the psyche is inevitable). His wife unexpectedly *crossed water* (first contact of the conscious with the subconscious), but when the two women in the Captain's life happened to meet, they did not recognise one another (the two minds do not ordinarily know one another). While at sea, our *sailor* discusses the subject of happiness with his first mate and the script has him say: 'He who seeks *happiness* must first find the *golden key*'. Subsequently, there is a direct quotation about Prometheus 'bringing down fire' (a clear indication that the process has begun).

With the two women (the two minds), a gradual *reversal* of roles takes place, culminating in a total *upheaval* in the Captain's affairs. In North Africa, the hot, dry place so often utilised by allegorical writers, there is a violent quarrel (a *conflict*) which ends in a *death* of the taxi driver, whose name is *Absalom* (a son who rebelled against his *father*). This indicates the first stage of the process. In Gibraltar, a similar upheaval occurs. Finally, facing a self-inflicted death by execution, the Captain makes a further *sacrifice* by giving up everything he possesses in his former life and then staging his own death (final stage of the process). But although the rest of the world assumed him to be dead, in reality, he is resurrected in a completely *new life* (process complete).

I cannot with any authority state that Alec Coppel, the screen writer responsible for the production was in possession of Hermetic knowledge, for the idea for his storyline may well have originated from the plot of an earlier Hermetic work, and have been adapted to the twentieth century. Yet, the proliferation of initiate clues within the film script is both significant and remarkable.

The greatest problem confronting those wishing to become acquainted with Hermetic lore lies in the realisation that many of the code words, once recognised, have a meaning attached to them today which is different to that originally conceived. As an instance relevant to a chapter in this book we may select 'humility', as it is used in connection with the Plantagenet family name. On reading the word 'humility' in the present day there is a tendency to envisage an attitude of self-effacement or subservience – all the outward signs of penitence. But this is entirely erroneous, for the mental process is something which takes place in the mind alone and has little to do with the physical body's outward stance. The 'humility' in question, therefore, is a humility of mind, an acceptance of, a complete realisation of the spiritual poverty suffered by the self compared to the Self. It is an admission to oneself that there is a subconscious power, that there is a way to reach it, and that this power exceeds anything that the day to day mind can envisage. Further, it is not merely a question of making just a superficial admission to oneself, and *not really believing it*. The admission must be wholehearted.

As a final comment, I particularly emphasise the fact that the words 'meditation' and 'contemplation', descriptive of the mental process, have themselves been subject to latter day misinterpretation. I therefore warn all those who would take up the practice to be certain that they can differentiate between true Meditation and that dangerous state which is no more than idle introversion.

I have no doubts whatsoever that many will find themselves unable to believe that the Hermetic 'code' as I have expressed it is anything more than synchronicity. To those, I leave a last quotation from Madame Blavatsky, who in *Isis Unveiled* significantly stated:

> Too many of our thinkers do not consider that the numerous changes in language, the allegorical phraseology and evident secretiveness of old Mystic writers, who were generally under an obligation never to divulge the solemn secrets of the sanctuary, might have sadly misled translators and commentators. The phrases of the mediaeval alchemists they read literally; and even the veiled symbology of Plato is commonly misunderstood by the modern scholar. One day they may *learn to know better*.

Bibliography

Blavatsky, H.P.: *Isis Unveiled* Vols I & II, Theosophical University Press USA, 1972

Cooper-Oakley, Isabel: *The Count of Saint Germain*, Rudolph Steiner Publications, USA, 1970

Defoe, Daniel: *Robinson Crusoe*, Everyman Library, 1970

Haggard, H. Rider: *She*, Macdonald, 1969

Hugo, V.: *The Hunchback of Notre Dame*, Collins Classics, 1953

Josephus, Flavius: *The Jewish Wars*, Heinman, 1926

More, Louis T.: *Robert Boyle* (biography), Oxford University Press, 1944

Shelley, Mary: *Frankenstein*, Oxford University Press, 1969

Sylvester, R.S.: *The Complete Works of Thomas More*, Yale University Press, 1963

Westfall, R.: *Never at Rest* (Newton biography), Cambridge University Press, 1980